Cheers for *Tough Calls*

"*Tough Calls* is a relevant and practical read that succinctly addresses everyday stressors in the life of a leader. It engaged me both as a minister and as a Christian leader striving to make a difference in corporate America."
—**Craig Harwood,** *human resources, Coca-Cola Company*

"As a highly successful pastor of a largely urban church congregation, Travis Collins has consolidated his years of experience in officiating high school football into a how-to book on leadership. Had I read these principles prior to my 54 years of leadership in higher education, I could have been a more effective and constructive leader."
—**Dr. E. Bruce Heilman,** *chancellor, University of Richmond*

"Call time-out! Request a review by the referee. This 'tough call' by pastor and football official Travis Collins deserves every camera angle possible. It is authentic, filled with wisdom, and just plain makes sense."
—**Dan Yeary,** *pastor, North Phoenix Baptist Church*

"Based on Christian values and supported by leadership scholarship, *Tough Calls* offers the reader more than just a quick-fix approach to decision making. At times humorous and always insightful, this book is an enjoyable and enlightening read."
—**Dr. Anne W. Perkins**
professor of leadership studies, Christopher Newport University

TOUGH
CALLS

**GAME-WINNING PRINCIPLES FOR
LEADERS UNDER PRESSURE**

BY TRAVIS COLLINS

NEW HOPE
PUBLISHERS
Birmingham, Alabama

New Hope® Publishers
P. O. Box 12065
Birmingham, AL 35202-2065
www.newhopepublishers.com

New Hope® Publishers is a division of WMU®.

Library of Congress Cataloging-in-Publication Data

Collins, Travis.
  Tough calls : game-winning principles for leaders under pressure /
by Travis Collins.
    p. cm.
  ISBN 978-1-59669-229-9 (sc)
  1. Christian leadership. I. Title.
  BV652.1.C64 2008
  253--dc22
                        2008016463

All Scripture quotations, unless otherwise indicated, are taken from the HOLY BIBLE, NEW INTERNATIONAL VERSION®. NIV®. Copyright © 1973, 1978, 1984 by International Bible Society. Used by permission of Zondervan. All rights reserved.

Scripture quotations marked (KJV) are taken from The Holy Bible, King James Version.

Scripture quotations marked (NASB) are taken from the New American Standard Bible®, Copyright © 1960, 1962, 1963, 1968, 1971, 1972, 1973, 1975, 1977, 1995 by the Lockman Foundation. Used by permission.

Cover design by Brand Navigation, brandnavigation.com
Interior design by Sherry Hunt

ISBN-10:1-59669-229-4
ISBN-13: 978-1-59669-229-9
N084149 • 0908 • 4M1

*Dedicated to my friends
and colleagues of the Central Virginia
Football Officials Association*

Table of Contents

Introduction: Pregame Warm-up 9

Section One: Tough Calls

1. Tough Calls 16
2. A Touchdown on the 5-yard Line 23
3. "Call It Both Ways, Ref" 29
4. Stick to Your Call and Be Patient 37
5. Sometimes the Call Has to Be Reversed 44

Section Two: This Ain't Easy

6. Battle Scars 50
7. This Ain't Easy. 57
8. Change Is Painful. 62

Section Three: Poise

9. Poise Means. 72
10. Under Control 80
11. The Roots of Poise 84
12. More Roots of Poise 91

Section Four: Criticism and Conflict

13. Don't Take It Personally 102
14. Unmet Expectations 109
15. Dealing with Criticism. 115
16. Worth Fighting For 125

Section Five: People Issues

17. You Gotta Call Unsportsmanlike Conduct 132
18. Handling Troublemakers 138
19. When People Disqualify Themselves 147

Section Six: More People Issues

20. There's a Time and a Place 160
21. Who's in Charge Here? 165
22. Leading Without the White Hat 171
23. Stress on the Family 178

Section Seven: A Mind-set

24. "My First Step Is Back" 186
25. Kindness Goes a Long Way 191
26. Moving On 197
27. Make the Call—It's Your Job 204

Conclusion: The Closing Minutes 211

Discussion Questions 217

INTRODUCTION

Pregame Warm-up

The book you just picked up is about spiritual leadership in difficult situations, no matter whether those situations occur in a secular workplace or a Christian organization. These pages are for those of us who genuinely want to lead spiritually—to reflect the character of Jesus in the way that we influence people— regardless of where or who we are leading.

Some of you are exercising spiritual leadership in public schools or political offices, in financial institutions or retail businesses, in manufacturing plants or on athletic teams. Others are exercising spiritual leadership in churches, non-profit organizations, social ministries, or in Christian media. Some of you have formal leadership titles; others don't have the titles, yet you are the ones to whom people look for direction. I'm writing this for all of us who want our leadership to reflect our faith commitments, and I write with the conviction that all of us can learn to lead more effectively.

Many of you lead in arenas far larger and more complex, and in many ways different, from anything I have known. I don't pretend to understand the pressures and responsibilities that you face. Yet, as a pastor and fellow leader, it would be my honor if you would journey with me through this book, learning to build your leadership practices on Christian principles.

The recurring theme of this book is the correlation between leadership and sports—sports officiating in particular. I was struck by the similarities between the worlds of athletics and leadership as soon as I began officiating high school football several years ago. Jesus used parables to relate truth to common life, and I've tried to do something similar by relating the challenges of leadership to the challenges of officiating athletic contests.

What Is Spiritual Leadership?

I want to be clear about three of my assumptions at the outset:

1. Leadership is not about who holds the loftiest title in an organization. One definition of leadership (and one I like), is simply "influence." You can, and ought to, influence the behavior and thinking of others whether you are the so-called boss or not.

2. Spiritual leadership is not only for pastors and others in vocational ministry. By spiritual leadership I mean influencing people as we act according to spiritual principles—specifically, those principles that accurately reflect the character of Jesus. Jesus was grounded in His relationship to the Father, and that bond is the underpinning of Jesus's perfect leadership. Of course we will never do anything perfectly like Jesus did. Yet, via our own relationship to the Father, through Jesus, we all can be truly spiritual leaders.

3. These spiritual principles—the leadership qualities of Jesus—include the following (and you probably will think of others):

- **The spiritual leader is willing to forgo self-seeking goals for the sake of the organization.** "I am the good shepherd. The good shepherd lays down his life for the sheep" (John 10:11).
- **The spiritual leader is a person of integrity.** "Simply let your 'Yes' be 'Yes,' and your 'No,' 'No'" (Matthew 5:37).
- **People are more important than the spiritual leader's plans.** "Then little children were brought to Jesus for him to place his hands on them and pray for them. But the disciples rebuked those who brought them. Jesus said, 'Let the little children come to me, and do not hinder them, for the kingdom of heaven belongs to such as these'" (Matthew 19:13–14).
- **The spiritual leader has a sense of divinely ordained mission and will not turn aside from that mission.** "I must be about my Father's business" (Luke 2:49 KJV).
- **The spiritual leader is willing to endure criticism, even from those close to him or her.** "Woe to you when all men speak well of you." (Luke 6:26). "When his family heard about this, they went to take charge of him, for they said, 'He is out of his mind'" (Mark 3:21).
- **The spiritual leader cannot live to meet others' expectations.** "The people were looking for him and when they came to where he was, they tried to keep him from leaving them. But he said, 'I must preach the good news of the kingdom of

God to the other towns also, because that is why I was sent'" (Luke 4:42–43).

- **Niceness is not the highest virtue.** "So he made a whip out of cords, and drove all from the temple...and overturned their tables" (John 2:15).
- **Confrontation is sometimes necessary.** "Woe to you, teachers of the law and Pharisees, you hypocrites!" (Matthew 23:27).
- **New approaches are often needed.** "Neither do men pour new wine into old wineskins" (Matthew 9:17).
- **The absence of conflict does not always signal a positive spiritual environment.** "I did not come to bring peace, but a sword" (Matthew 10:34).
- **Truly great spiritual leaders possess the unique combination of savvy and purity.** "Be as shrewd as snakes and as innocent as doves" (Matthew 10:16).
- **Strong leadership is servant leadership.** "He poured water into a basin and began to wash his disciples' feet" (John 13:5).

These qualities of Jesus's leadership underlie every page of this book. And when I use the word *effectiveness* in this book, I mean measuring results by how consistent they are with the life and teachings of Jesus. The yardstick is not the financial bottom line. In other words, I'm talking about emulating Jesus, not Donald Trump.

We can lead spiritually whether or not our context would be considered spiritual. And we can do so even in difficult situations. I write this with a prayer that in these pages you will find ideas to help you reflect the Spirit of Christ even in hard times. Ken Blanchard and company have helped us "lead like Jesus." My goal here is to help us make tough calls like Jesus.

About the <u>Just for Vocational Ministers</u> Sections

At the end of each chapter, there is a box in which I address those who serve in churches or other Christian ministry. If you are not a vocational minister, feel free to skip that box and go to the next chapter.

SECTION ONE
TOUGH CALLS

*Elijah went before the people and said,
"How long will you waver between two
opinions? If the LORD is God, follow
him; but if Baal is God, follow him."
But the people said nothing.*
—1 Kings 18:21

1

Tough Calls

I remember right where I was when I witnessed what NFL Films hailed as the greatest play in National Football League history—what many of us know as the "Immaculate Reception." It was 1972, and I was a 13-year-old sitting in Alan Thomason's living room watching the Pittsburgh Steelers and the Oakland Raiders in a thriller of a playoff game. The Steelers had the ball but were down 7–6 with less than 30 ticks of the clock left in the contest. Pay dirt was 60 long yards away.

Terry Bradshaw made a rather desperate throw to John "Frenchy" Fuqua. Fuqua, Jack Tatum of the Raiders, and the football arrived at the same place at the same time, and the ball ended up sailing back toward the line of scrimmage. The pass would fall incomplete, and the Steelers would go home losers.

Except.

Except Steeler Franco Harris happened to be running where the ball happened to be falling. He snatched the pigskin not far from his shoestrings and stumbled toward the goal line, eventually gaining his balance enough to race 42 yards and score the winning touchdown in one of the most celebrated games ever.

But wait.

Did the ball ricochet off the hands of Pittsburgh's Fuqua directly to the hands of his teammate, Franco Harris? If so, the pass should have been declared incomplete, because the rule in those days stated that two offensive receivers could not touch a pass unless a defender had touched it in between. The officials conferred and, based on what the official closest to the play reported, referee Fred Swearingen ruled it a catch. He signaled a touchdown.

People still argue over what the replay shows. Did the defender, Tatum, actually touch the ball, or did he just hit Fuqua? It happened so fast. And in those days instant replay was not used to reconsider the call of the officials on the field. It was a tough call; nobody denied that. Yet no one was feeling sorry for the officials. One of the responsibilities of an official is to make a call and live with it—even when the stakes are high. Even when it is a tough call.

Officials and Leadership

I know about tough football calls. Several times a week during the fall I don my striped shirt and my knickers, put my yellow flag in my pocket and my whistle around my neck, and take the football field. Granted, I'm not exactly in the National Football League (NFL); a fierce high school rivalry is as big-time as it gets for me. Even so, my games can get intense. In fact, if you really want to see intense, come with me to a flag football game—the game for the little kids—and listen to the coaches and parents!

Every time I walk on the field as an official, I am putting myself in a potentially confrontational, argumentative, tense, and all-around-nasty situation. It's as if my zebra shirt has a sign on it that reads, *If you're unhappy with the way things go here, feel free to let me know. Passionately.*

If you are a leader you probably are beginning to see the connection between officiating and leadership. If you haven't yet seen the parallels, maybe the following quote, from *Psychology of Officiating* by professors Robert S. Weinberg and Peggy A. Richardson, will help: "Officiating can be challenging, exciting, and rewarding. On the other hand, officials can also feel frustrated, abused, and unappreciated."

We could easily substitute *leadership* and *leaders,* for *officiating* and *officials* in that quote. If you are a leader, you undoubtedly have noted the connection by now. The theme of this book is that both spiritual leadership and sports officiating require tough calls. Both leaders and sports officials have to make hard decisions and live with them. Living with the hard decisions includes taking the heat from those who disagree, and, on occasion, it means acknowledging the humbling reality that we've missed a call.

The ability to make tough calls is a key component of good leadership. Yet we shouldn't assume that only a chosen few are able to do so. Everyone can learn to make better, more courageous, more prudent decisions. If you are completely unable to make tough calls, quite frankly, I wonder whether you ought to be in a leadership role. But if your leadership is confirmed in other areas, and you feel like decision making is simply one of your weaknesses (and we all have our weaknesses), then perhaps this book will help you.

Why I Wrote This Book

I believe God prompted me to research this topic so that I would be prepared to make some difficult decisions that I could not have anticipated at the time I began this project. Since I started work on this book I've had to make some tough calls. Even as I type these words I am only a few weeks beyond making one of the toughest calls I've ever faced. I got good counsel from wise people, but sound advice does not remove the angst of hard decisions.

Over the years I've made a number of tough calls as a spiritual leader:

- Tough calls, the majority of which went unnoticed by most people.
- Tough calls that have affected people's vocations.
- Tough calls, one of which literally made me sick to my stomach.
- Tough calls, some of which turned out really well, and some of which didn't.

I'm OK with those tough calls, however, for they come with the calling to leadership. In fact, I would have a hard time holding my head up, and sleeping at night, if I were unwilling to make the difficult decisions. The late Earl Strom, an excellent long-time National Basketball Association (NBA) official, wrote this about tough calls:

I was taught from the beginning, and it has stuck with me through all these years, that it's much easier to fight your way out of a place than to have to go look in the mirror and admit you backed down from a tough call.
—*Calling the Shots*, with Blaine Johnson

I know there are a lot of leadership books out there, and I have benefited from a number of them. Such important topics as vision, mission, teamwork, and strategy are treated in detail by those helpful tomes. Yet I want to offer something more; I want to offer encouragement to those leaders who are enduring unfair criticism, being second-guessed, and wondering if the opportunity before them is worth the risk. I want to offer observations that I pray will be helpful to those of you who are at the helms of ships sailing through, or toward, the storms.

Some surely will wonder why I think I know enough about leadership to write a book. It's rather sobering to think that people I have led (some of whose expectations I didn't meet) might actually read this. Nevertheless, this is a book I felt I had to write, for spiritual leadership is increasingly difficult, and we all need all the help we can get. Our rapidly changing culture tests the wills and skills of spiritual leaders, whether you are a school administrator, a denominational leader, a warehouse manager, a lay leader in your church, a corporate executive, a pastor, or the captain of your team. I hope from my experience—including my mistakes—in officiating and spiritual leadership you can mine some nuggets of truth that will benefit you.

Franco and Physics

Back to the so-called Immaculate Reception for a moment.... There was so much continuous controversy surrounding Franco Harris's amazing catch that nearly three decades later a Carnegie Mellon physics professor, John Fetkovich, was asked to investigate. He was charged with determining whether Tatum (the defender) or Fuqua (the intended receiver) touched the ball before Harris caught it. Remember that, according to the NFL rules in 1971, had two offensive receivers in a row touched the pass, the pass should have been ruled incomplete.

Fetkovich determined the officials correctly ruled that Tatum (the defender) touched the ball. The scientist postulated that for the ball to have bounced back toward the line of scrimmage as far as it did, it had to have been propelled by the only body (Tatum's) that was headed in that direction. In short, Fetkovich's findings confirmed that the officials got it right.

History and instant replay prove that good officials make the right call far more often than the wrong one. The same is true of good leaders. If you are a true leader, you are going to make the right decision most of the time.

If you are a follower of Jesus and the Creator of the universe has called you into leadership, then you can be confident. God's Spirit lives in you and works through you, and you have those God-given instincts that guide your decision making even when information is insufficient. However, we still need to work hard at becoming the most gutsy, skilled, astute call-makers we can be. In the pages to come we'll look deeper at this critical topic.

Just for Vocational Ministers

Leadership in any setting is hard, and leadership in Christian ministry is particularly demanding. Many who work in Christian organizations, for example, are working mostly with volunteers, and that demands leadership by persuasion, without the leverage of a payday. And when it comes to supervision, my hunch is that we vocational ministers are among the most complicated supervisees in the world. Furthermore, the abuse leaders sometimes receive at church seems to hurt worse than abuse in other places, for we expect more from our fellow Christians.

I've served either as a pastor or a missionary since 1984. I currently serve as senior pastor at Bon Air Baptist Church in Richmond, Virginia. By including these special notes, I want to assist and encourage vocational ministers who may be suffering through a particularly difficult stretch of the vocational ministry road. May God use the words on these pages to strengthen you, my colleagues, as you make the tough calls.

2

A Touchdown on the 5-yard Line

Officials don't always get it right. Sometimes those fans who sit in their easy chairs and scream at their televisions have legitimate gripes. Sometimes the coaches are correct when they zealously suggest to an official that he missed a call. Although I'm writing from the perspective of an official and acknowledge my bias toward those who officiate the games, I admit that we sometimes goof. For example...

It was early in my first year as an official. At an important moment in the contest the offensive team was down around the 9-yard line and driving. The offense could smell the end zone, and I was on high alert.

A touchdown is the most exciting moment of a football game, of course, and so when I call a touchdown I want to call it with authority. They taught us in the training program not to be tentative. "When you make a call, make it!" they told us. "Sell it!"

The ball was handed off to a strapping fullback, and I saw him carry the ball across the line, with two or three defenders in tow. Standing astride the line I raised my arms strong and straight to signal a touchdown and blew my whistle loud enough for folks in the next county to hear me.

But then…

The players just turned and looked at me with a puzzled look on their faces. My heart sank. Something was wrong. I looked down at my feet…and I was standing on the 5-yard line.

Was that embarrassing? What do you think?

But I've realized something—people who are afraid they might call a touchdown on the 5-yard line never know the joy of calling touchdowns at all. People who are afraid to make mistakes never take risks. This book is about leadership, and leaders who fear risk will be weak, ineffective leaders. If our confidence is so fragile that we can't risk looking bad, we will be too guarded to lead effectively.

Leaders Can't Fear Risk

When our oldest son was in high school, his football team's motto one year was: "I am not afraid of failure. I *am* afraid of mediocrity." Any good leader is going to embrace that philosophy. People who are afraid to risk failure are doomed to mediocre results.

I've studied leadership for a long time, and I've watched some pretty good spiritual leaders up close. I've even stumbled around in the role of leader myself for a while. One thing I've noticed is that every venture does not pan out, no matter how noble the intentions of the leader, how thorough the plan, or how great the potential of the endeavor. I've seen leaders' decisions go bad and watched followers question those leaders' credibility. I've seen ventures fail and watched organizations pay a high price in terms of finances, personnel, and harmony. I've even seen leaders lose their positions because gambles didn't pay off.

Yet I have watched far more groups flounder because of tentativeness. I've seen organizations plateau simply because the leaders seemed more interested in popularity and job security than in fulfilling a mission. I've even seen churches slowly die, ironically, because no one seemed willing to risk. Mistakes caused by poor preparation and reckless leadership are inexcusable. But mistakes of initiative are not only forgivable, they are downright commendable.

I am not championing capriciousness. Whimsical, foolish leadership is hazardous. I'm calling for prayerfully deliberate risk. The goal is a balance between danger and discretion. If we don't risk, and even make mistakes, we won't be doing much. Successful, effective people make a lot of mistakes.

The Right Mistakes

Of course we don't want to make foolish, catastrophic mistakes. We want to make the *right* mistakes.

Writing with Dave Kaplan in *When You Come to a Fork in the Road, Take It,* famous Yankee catcher Yogi Berra relates a great anecdote about mistakes. When the Pittsburgh Pirates stunned the sports world by beating his New York Yankees in the 1960 World Series, a reporter asked Yogi how the unthinkable happened. Yogi answered, "We made too many wrong mistakes." Typical Yogi Berra. And his implication (a correct one, I might add) is that there are *right* mistakes.

Since I took on the role of senior pastor at Bon Air Baptist Church in 2002, we have embarked on some ventures that didn't meet expectations. Yet I believe that in retrospect they can be deemed right mistakes. They were the right mistakes, because we knew the potential risks going in. They were the right mistakes, because they didn't utterly jeopardize the church's health. And they were the right mistakes, because they were attempted so that lives would be transformed.

I understand that if I lead folks out on too many limbs that break, limb climbing will get mighty unpopular around our church. Yet I cannot allow myself to be paralyzed by fear of future failure. When I become a lily-livered leader, the organization is going to be in trouble.

When the inevitable failures occur, we absolutely must choose to move on. Both Ned and Dan Wilford, twin brothers, were long-time college football officials. Dan also went on to officiate in the NFL. Writing with Stephen Byrum in their book *You Threw the Flag*, Dan shares Ned's philosophy on mistakes:

> *I have heard Ned asked the question of what was his biggest mistake in a ball game. He pauses and thinks as seriously as he can. He is sure that he has made mistakes, but he simply cannot remember any....He believes that since mistakes cannot be undone and since they are an inevitable part of the whole big picture of life, that they are best forgotten. He so strongly embraces this philosophy that his mind keeps drawing a blank on bad calls that he may have made.*

Since the inevitable mistakes of life cannot be retracted, revoked, or rescinded, Wilford is right: they shouldn't be forever regretted. It is a truism that we must learn from our mistakes. Certainly, if we don't learn from them we repeat them. Yet we must not drag the memories of those mistakes around like a ball and chain.

My touchdown call on the 5-yard line reminds me how important it is to know where I am on the field when I signal a touchdown. Somewhere down inside my subconscious there is probably a warning that goes off every time I prepare to raise my arms and blow the whistle: Stop! Look around! Make sure you know where you are! Yet the memory of my blunder hasn't paralyzed me to the point that I can't call a touchdown when I see one. Likewise, as a leader, I cannot allow myself to be hamstrung by excess caution, for more failure has resulted from faintheartedness than from audacity.

Just for Vocational Ministers

Steve and Shelly McCord, members of my church, brought me a book autographed by Erwin McManus, cultural architect and lead pastor of Mosaic in Los Angeles. They are former members of his church, and they know how much I admire his work. In the front he had written, "To Travis—Risk everything!"

Risk everything!

Everything?!

Maybe one day I'll have the chance to ask Erwin exactly what he meant by everything. In the meantime, I think I get his point: leadership of a church, or any Christian organization, is risky business. Not only are the health and future of the organization at stake; eternal destinies hang in the balance. Fulfilling our mission as God's people requires risk.

The Lord of the Church once told the story of a man who hid his talent so as not to risk losing it. That timid investor was the goat, not the hero, of the story. I think that tells us what Jesus thinks of risk.

Maybe Erwin is right.

3

"Call It Both Ways, Ref"

Former NBA official Tim Donaghy was at the center of one of the biggest scandals in the history of American professional sports. In the summer of 2007 Donaghy resigned his NBA position just prior to revelations from an FBI investigation that charged him with illegal gambling activity. According to court documents, he bet on NBA games and gave bettors inside information. He pleaded guilty to two felony charges the FBI leveled against him.

This one crooked official temporarily undermined the integrity of a professional sport and jeopardized the reputation of every official of every sport. If there is one thing we demand of officials, it is fairness.

Good coaches, players, and fans expect nothing more than evenhandedness. Of course, given their preferences, they'd like the judgment calls to go their way. But I think most folks, deep down inside, expect nothing more than an impartially called game.

Integrity Is...

Integrity is non-negotiable for leaders. You can lack many skills and still excel as a leader, but you cannot lead well without integrity. Integrity means saying what is true, doing what you say, and living out your convictions. If you are a person of integrity, people can expect you to act and speak in the same manner no matter the circumstance. Your behavior grows out of, and is consistent with, your true character. Even those who oppose you will respect you if you act with integrity. In countless situations people have given a leader the benefit of the doubt, because they trusted his or her heart.

It takes a lot of courage to do the right thing when to do so is costly. I believe the bottom line in all matters of integrity is courage—courage to stick to what is true and just, even when a high price must be paid. Psalm 15:4 describes the person of integrity as one who "keeps his oath even when it hurts." If you want the people you lead to be committed and loyal, then be genuine and truthful. In the words of Jesus, "simply let your 'Yes' be 'Yes,' and your 'No,' 'No'" (Matthew 5:37).

Integrity is a multifaceted characteristic of good spiritual leaders. Integrity means:

- **Consistency**

Consistency is imperative in officiating. If people notice that the ref is letting the red team get away with unfair play but is calling one penalty after another on the blue team, then his reputation for fairness is at risk. If the umpire is giving one pitcher the corners, but not giving them to the opposing pitcher, people are going to cry foul!

Consistency is no less critical in spiritual leadership. If your position on an issue depends on to whom you are speaking, or if certain folks are getting preferential treatment because of their bank statements or their titles, then you are on the verge of forfeiting your leadership.

Furthermore, one of the difficult aspects of leadership is that those tough calls just keep on comin'. Leadership does not allow us to make a couple of dazzling decisions and then coast. Leadership demands constant, consistent decision making.

NFL umpire, Art Demmas, told me that prior to a Raiders game one day, he was with Art McNally (then the supervisor of NFL officials) when they ran into legendary coach John Madden. McNally asked Madden, "Do you know Art Demmas?"

Coach Madden answered, "Yeah, I know Demmas; he's a good umpire!"

Demmas replied, "Coach, that's pretty much on a game-to-game basis, isn't it?"

"No, Art," said Madden, "that's on a *play-to-play* basis."

Your leadership, too, is judged on a play-to-play, decision-to-decision, relationship-to-relationship basis. Consistency is critical.

- **Fairness (Justice)**

You can't help but like some people you lead more than others, but you can decide that you will treat everyone fairly. Personal preferences must never result in playing favorites.

By the way, have you ever wondered if berating an official hurts or helps a team's cause? Does calling the referee a blind idiot maximize the likelihood that the next judgment call will go your way? Or does it make him so mad that you won't be able to get a judgment call the rest of the night? I guess it depends on the official. Of course, ideally, whether or not you tell him he's a blind idiot shouldn't make a bit of difference in the rest of his calls. But officials, after all, are human. Why, even *judges* are human.

In *My City Was Gone*, Dennis Love recounts the fascinating story of a $700 million lawsuit in my hometown of Anniston, Alabama. *Abernathy vs. Monsanto* was a complex case involving thousands of townspeople who wanted damages from the Monsanto Company, which was ultimately found to be legally responsible for unbelievable pollution of the local area. Circuit Judge Joel Laird, an outspoken Christian, presided over the legal circus. Quite frankly, he found it hard not to get ticked off at the company's team of defense lawyers. Their high-and-mighty attitude got under his skin. The overbearing barristers often seemed downright antagonistic toward the good judge. How did he handle that?

"I'm human," Laird later admitted. "People try not to be human and pretend that things don't bother them. But I am what I am and I'm comfortable with that. I was bothered by it. But it just made me more determined to be as fair and impartial as I could be and keep everything on track."

Laird was honest; being evenhanded sometimes requires gritting our teeth and treating everyone fairly even when it hurts. Good judges do it, though. Good sports officials do it. Good leaders do it, too.

- **Wholeness**

Integrity comes from the same root as the word *integer*, or whole number. A person of integrity is whole, not divided; he or she is the same, no matter the location and no matter who is present. Integrity earns the admiration of others, and puts the one practicing it at ease. There is a calm assurance—a deep self-respect—that comes from being whole.

At the heart of integrity is a strong identity. Wholeness results from knowing who we are—being comfortable, as some have put it, in our skin. The leader who is whole has decided what is important to him or her, and is guided by a deep sense of purpose. The leader who is whole has consciously chosen the path that his or her life will take, has wrestled with the moral questions of life, and determined his or her values and convictions. Thus wholeness—living out one's identity—comes naturally; the leader rarely has to even think about it. And even in those rare situations when the leader is tempted to compromise his or her convictions, this wholeness—this consistency of identity—reminds the leader of values far too important to sacrifice on the altar of expediency.

Integrity's Rewards

Let me remind you of the rewards of integrity. First, God is delighted. God doesn't take kindly to dishonesty, but He takes great joy in truthfulness. "The Lord detests lying lips, but he delights in men who are truthful" (see Proverbs 11:1; 12:22). God beams with Dad-like pride when we make tough, but honest, choices.

Second, your reputation sparkles. In 2 Kings 12:15 we read, "They did not require an accounting from those to whom they gave the money to pay the workers, because they acted with complete honesty." If you develop a reputation for honesty, people will say of you, "If he says it you can believe it." That is true not only in business, but in personal relationships as well. When you and I are honest, people trust our hearts. If you want to have close friends, and if you want people to trust you even when they disagree with you or misunderstand you, then always be honest.

Of course it takes a while to earn that reputation. Umpire Dave Phillips, who spent 32 years in the Major Leagues, writes:

> A good reputation is perhaps the most important intangible an umpire can possess. The hardest part about it is, you have to earn it. There is no other way to get it. You can't walk into Kmart and buy credibility. If you could, every new umpire would be standing in line when the store opened.
>
> —*Center Field on Fire*, with Rob Rains

A third reward of integrity is that you can rest well. "The integrity of the upright guides them, but the unfaithful are destroyed by their duplicity" (Proverbs 11:3). Duplicity haunts us.

There is a great scene in the movie *The Legend of Bagger Vance* that illustrates my point. Junuh, the hometown golfing hero of Savannah, Georgia, is preparing to take his shot on the final hole of the final round of a tournament in which he's competing against the two best golfers of the era. He is about to take a shot from the fairway, and as he moves a twig from in front of the ball, the ball rolls just a bit. Tournament rules state that when the ball moves, the player is charged with a one-stroke penalty. Junuh and the other two golfers are tied, it is the last hole, and a one-stroke penalty will almost certainly destroy Junuh's chances of winning. Junuh is playing for respect, not just money, so this hole is huge.

TOUGH CALLS

"The ball moved," Junuh says quietly.

"No," says Hardy, Junuh's ten-year-old admirer, standing nearby.

"It moved," Junuh repeats. "I have to call a stroke on myself."

Junuh begins to walk toward the judge to tell him the ball moved, and so he will have to take a stroke penalty.

Hardy runs and catches him. "No! No! Don't do it!" Hardy pleads, for Hardy wants his hero to win this tournament so badly he can taste it. "*Please* don't do it! Only you and me seen it, and I won't tell a soul. Cross my heart. Ain't nobody gonna know."

"*I* will, Hardy," Junuh answers. "And so will *you*."

Junuh was right; we never get away with a lie, even when we think we've forgotten. Every act of dishonesty hides away in our heart and lies there apparently unknown. All the while, however, those forgotten-but-restless skeletons in the closets of our hearts make us uneasy. We feel badly about ourselves, our self-respect suffers, and we don't even know why.

So be honest, be consistent, and keep your word. Then lie down and get a good night's sleep.

Let's simply decide to be people of integrity. You can decide today: "I will not be dishonest even about the little things. I will not exaggerate. I will not hedge. I will be honest even when it is to my disadvantage. I will be evenhanded." It's simple, really. Don't lie. Don't cheat. Don't dance around the truth. Be honest. Be fair. Be the same in every situation.

You and I can say, as did Job, *"As long as I have life within me, the breath of God in my nostrils, my lips will not speak wickedness, and my tongue will utter no deceit . . . till I die, I will not deny my integrity"* (Job 27:3–4).

Just for Vocational Ministers

Integrity is the result of a *decision* to be completely and deliberately honest in all situations. In *Leaders on Leadership*, George Barna writes, "A leader's commitment to walk with integrity of heart calls for a refusal to allow even minor deviations from honesty of any kind." This means no exaggerations, even in the slightest.

"Few things," Barna continues, "are more important to the character of a leader than exhibiting absolute honesty in all communication with those whom he leads. Often we face the temptation to exaggerate numbers, such as church attendance figures."

Did I just hear someone say, "Ouch!"?

4

Stick to Your Call
and Be Patient

A leader can easily flaunt his or her convictions when things are going well. But when the outcome still hangs in the balance—when the results are not yet clear and people are questioning the plans—a leader's resolve is tested.

When a football official makes a judgment call, a few tense ticks of the clock follow during which he might be tempted to change that call. On a pass play, for example, he throws a flag in the vicinity of the defensive back. Coaches, players, and fans immediately clamor, "You can't call that! That was not interference!" He second-guesses himself. *Maybe they're right,* he thinks. *Maybe that was incidental contact. Maybe I've just thrown a foolish flag.* For a moment he considers picking up his flag and putting it back in his pocket. That is particularly tempting for inexperienced officials. The good official, however, will stick to his call.

Do good officials ever reverse their decisions? Certainly, when a reversal is warranted. But when a solid official has seen something clearly he will not reverse his decision, no matter how intense the pressure. In the same way, when a strong leader is convinced that he or she is leading the organization in the right direction, the leader will not change directions, even when the early results do not confirm the leader's call.

Don't Give Up on Your Vision

In 1983, his third year as the Duke men's basketball coach, Mike Krzyzewski, "Coach K," led his team to a disappointing 11-17 record. A lot of folks were down on Duke, convinced this guy with the funny last name had been the wrong choice. But Coach K stuck with his plan, and three years later Duke was 37-3 and made it to the final game of the National Collegiate Athletic Association (NCAA) championship tournament. He has since won three NCAA championships at Duke. In *Leading with the Heart*, with Donald T. Phillips, Coach K writes about the courage of convictions:

> *True bravery in leadership really revolves around the degree to which a person maintains the courage of his convictions. That kind of courage takes persistence to keep believing in yourself—and resilience to keep picking yourself up after every loss, every stumble, every fall. Following through with your plans, your commitments, your dreams—even when everyone else is saying you can't do it—that's courage.*

In 1996, Tony Dungy, a devoted follower of Jesus, became head coach of the Tampa Bay Buccaneers. Expectations were high, but the Bucs lost their first five games. Some around him were questioning if he knew what he was doing. Nevertheless

TOUGH CALLS

Coach Dungy was convinced he had to model perseverance even in the hard times. And he did. Believing that he had discerned God's plan, Dungy was patient.

"You have to be willing to stick with God's plan even when you don't understand it," says Dungy in *God Is My CEO* by Larry Julian.

After the dismal start, the Bucs won 6 of their final 11 games that first year under Dungy. The next year, Dungy took the franchise to its first winning season in 15 years. In 2002, he became the Indianapolis Colts' head coach, and, in 2007, he led them to a Super Bowl victory over the Chicago Bears. His autobiography *Quiet Strength* is now a national best seller. He never would have attained such heights had he not remained tenaciously committed to his vision, even when others questioned it.

At one point in my leadership I sensed deeply that God was prompting our church to move in a specific direction—to launch multiple new campuses for our congregation and become a multi-site church. The leaders of the church expressed that they were sensing the same thing. Everyone in the church wasn't on board however. One lady (who is no longer in the church) registered her lack of confidence in me with these words: "I see where you're taking the train, and when you get there you're going to look back and see that no one is on board."

I took her warning seriously, for I realize that a person is not a leader unless people are following. And I've gotta admit, when we had a couple of fine families walk out, I thought the train might indeed be emptying. Yet I was as convinced as a human can be that God had spoken and that we were following His direction. So I pressed on, with the blessing of the church's lay leadership, and tried to be patient. Despite this lady's prediction, I believed the church was doing the right thing.

Some years have passed now, and there are more people on the train than when we started out in this direction. Some of those new to the train have experienced dramatic life transformation because we came this way. We never would have gotten here, however, had we turned back on the vision I believe God gave our church.

Patience Is a Virtue

We live in an impatient culture, and, often, we are most impatient with ourselves. If we are going to fulfill God's purposes for our lives—whether we are pastors, plumbers, or pediatricians—then we are going to have to commit to the long haul, not just the here-and-now, and understand the importance of patience.

Patience is certainly not my strong suit. *Im*patience, in fact, is in my genes. One of our well-worn family stories is of Uncle Bill Collins and the boat motor. Uncle Bill was a warm and loving man, but he had the patience (the *im*patience, rather) of a Collins. He and my dad were fishing one day on Alabama's Coosa River, and Uncle Bill had been having trouble with his boat motor all day long. His patience, what little there was to begin with, was running out. They decided to move from the spot where they were fishing, so Uncle Bill tried to crank his motor. He pulled the cord and yanked the cord, but the motor refused to start. He got so aggravated, so rankled, that he invented a few colorful phrases, unscrewed the clamp that held the uncooperative motor to the side of the boat, threw the motor into the river, and paddled to shore.

One day you are going to find yourself in danger of losing your patience in the middle of a leadership river. In those nerve-racking moments you are going to have to choose to be patient with people and with God. Or else you might find yourself up the creek without a motor.

A wise friend, Tom Jasper, once told me about greyhound racing dogs. In order to spur the dogs to run, Tom explained, a mechanical rabbit is placed in front of them. That mechanical rabbit stays out in front of the dogs throughout the race as an enticement, a goal, if you will. The dogs chase that rabbit to the finish line. (Of course they never catch it, which must make for some awfully neurotic greyhounds.)

If the rabbit ever gets too far out in front, the dogs will quit running. They will decide the goal is simply not achievable. The objective of those who operate the dog track is to keep the rabbit just a few feet ahead so that the dogs will want to catch it, but not so far out in front that they quit.

Likewise, Tom noted, a leader can't get too far out in front of his or her followers. If a vision is enticing, challenging, and not too far beyond their reach, then people will work hard for its fulfillment. If it seems too far out, however, people will simply give up, and the leader will turn around to see that no one is following.

My insightful friend made a good point—a point all spiritual leaders must heed. You will feel passionately about a particular project. You will send forth the call to charge a particular hill. You will put announcements in the company newsletter. You will invite people to join you in the noble adventure. Then, much to your disappointment, people will be slow to respond. Some will even yawn.

That's when you will have to discipline yourself to be patient. You might have to bring up your idea a few times before people buy into it. You might have to explain it several times before people can get their heads around it. But be patient; don't get so far out in front of people that they dismiss your vision.

Waiting on God

You will pray and believe that this project will be good for the organization and good for the world. Your sense of rightness will be deep and certain. The timing will seem right to you. And then, when things don't happen quickly, it will be easy to get discouraged.

Psalm 27:14 says, "Wait for the LORD; be strong and take heart and wait for the LORD." Patience with God means waiting on, trusting, and yielding control to our Father. God's timetable is different from ours. He doesn't seem to be in as much of a hurry as we do. For example:

- God promised Abraham a family that would be as numerous as the stars in the sky. Then he and Sarah had to wait until they were elderly to have their first and only child.
- God waited 40 years for the children of Israel to get their act together enough to take the Promised Land.
- God promised David a temple but God proved slower than present-day contractors in building the place.

- God took His time—waited for the alignment of transportation and language and religious hunger—before He became incarnate in Jesus. Then it was 30 years or so before Jesus began His public ministry.

God does not seem to be in a hurry.

Patience with God is faith in action, and waiting in hope brings its blessings. Isaiah 30:18 reads, "Yet the LORD longs to be gracious to you; he rises to show you compassion. For the LORD is a God of justice. Blessed are all who wait for him!"

When things aren't hopping and popping as you wish they were—when the project is taking too long to complete or events are unfolding far too slowly—don't lose your cool. When it seems like God is dragging His feet, be patient. I'm going to go out on a limb and suggest that God has better timing than you do.

Just for Vocational Ministers

Everyone won't share your vision, and I know that is frustrating. You will question people's dedication. You will wonder if people really love Jesus. You will lament the apathy epidemic. At that point you have two options. You can throw up your hands and cry, like Elijah under the juniper tree, "I am the only one left on earth who wants to serve God!" Or, you can be patient. And patience is nowhere more important than in the church.

5

Sometimes the Call Has to Be Reversed

An article in the March 2007 issue of *Referee* highlighted some of the all-time best calls in officiating history. Making the list was a significant call reversal by the umpiring crew during game six of the 2004 American League Championship Series.

It was the bottom of the eighth inning with the score Red Sox 4 Yankees 2. Yankee star Alex Rodriguez was at bat. A-Rod swung but barely made contact. The ball plopped out to the Boston pitcher, Bronson Arroyo, and it became a footrace to first. Umpire Randy Marsh's view of the play was obstructed by bodies, and what he saw, after Arroyo's attempted tag of Rodriguez, was the ball rolling free into the outfield. "Safe!" Marsh declared.

Marsh hadn't seen Rodriguez' intentional forearm blow to Arroyo's glove, knocking the ball loose. But two of the other umpires had seen it. They had a conference, and when other members of the umpiring crew reported Rodriguez's transgression, the crew decided to reverse the call. The umpires looked at each other and said, "Get ready, boys, because this place is gonna go nuts."

And nuts it went. When the umpires called A-Rod out, Yankee fans threw all kinds of trash from the stands, and their protests so disrupted the game that police had to position themselves around the field. Replays showed that the umpires did the right thing by reversing the call, but at the moment it looked like doing the right thing might result in a public stoning.

Getting It Right

Reversed calls often are a result of first-rate officiating. Another example of an appropriately reversed call provided one of the most memorable moments of recent NFL history.

If I say "tuck rule" many of you will think of Tom Brady and the New England Patriots. You probably can picture that 2002 American Football Conference (AFC) playoff game in the snow with the clock running out as Brady dropped back to pass, got hit by the Raiders' Charles Woodson, and lost the ball. Less than two minutes remained in the game, and the Patriots were down by three. When the Raiders fell on the football, it looked like the Patriots would be watching the rest of the playoffs from home. Walt Coleman, the referee, had ruled the play a fumble—Raiders' ball.

But hang on a second.

Coleman, along with the official in the booth, reviewed the play on the monitor and ruled that Brady had not yet tucked the ball against his body. Had Brady already brought the ball back to his chest, it would have been a fumble; but, since it was still untucked, it was ruled an incomplete forward pass.

That was the first time most of us had ever heard of the NFL's tuck rule. At any rate, Coleman reversed his own ruling and the Patriots maintained possession of the ball. They kicked a field goal to go into overtime and eventually won the game.

Fans and commentators across the country whined about the referee's call until we learned about the tuck rule, and then we whined about the tuck rule! While the rest of us were whining, by the way, the Patriots went on to win the Super Bowl and began a dynasty—thanks in part to a courageous official willing to reverse his decision.

Resolute or Just Plain Stubborn?

There is a fine line between determination and inflexibility. Solid convictions will keep the leader on course even when conventional wisdom says he or she is mistaken. A leader with strong beliefs will not be deterred by detractors, and such courage is admirable. That was my point in the previous chapter.

But what if a leader is just obstinate? What if he or she is demonstrating intransigence instead of courage? What one leader might call "resolve," everyone else might call "pigheadedness." How can we know the difference? In *Quiet Strength*, Tony Dungy quotes one of his mentors, Hall of Famer and former Steelers coach Chuck Noll, who said, "Being stubborn is a virtue when you're right; it's only a character flaw when you're wrong." So how do you know whether your dogged determination is a virtue or a character flaw?

The best way to determine whether a leader is being commendably resolute or just plain stubborn is to hear from others in the organization who (1) have bought into the organization's overall mission; (2) are positive people (not naysayers); (3) are loyal to the leadership; (4) are mature; and (5) have a good track record of wise decision making. If those people say it is time to change course, and the senior leader still insists on going his or her own way, the senior leader is probably just being mulish. If people are going to follow our lead, then they need to be confident that if we make a bad call, we will wave off the flag. We can change direction without sacrificing our mantle of leadership.

Note, however, that officials can lose the respect of fans and coaches if they wave off the flag too many times. Once in a game is no problem. People might even comment: "That's good officiating." Most folks are not likely to protest all that loudly even if the ref waves off his flag twice. An official who waves his flag too frequently, however, can wave the respect of fans, coaches, and even his fellow officials good-bye. Likewise, when a leader backs down, backs up, and backs off too often, he or she jeopardizes the confidence and support of his or her followers.

The truth remains, though, that calls occasionally need to be reversed, and good leaders aren't afraid to admit it. When leaders admit and rectify mistakes they not only increase the potential for their organization's success, they also send a couple of important signals: (1) the leader knows he or she isn't perfect; and (2) the organization is open to innovative, even risky, decisions.

Sometimes leaders need to wave off the flag or reverse the call. The willingness to say, "That did not go as well as planned," is a prerequisite of innovative, trustworthy leadership.

Just for Vocational Ministers

A few years ago our church decided to begin a Saturday night service. We did our homework, and I believe we paid attention as carefully as we could to the promptings of God's Spirit. For nearly two years that Saturday night service was effective. But then it was as if we had the sails up but the wind just wasn't blowing anymore. The service became a drain on the volunteers and the staff. Attendance began to slide. We went for a long stretch when we did not see any signs of significant life transformation. A number of really good things resulted from that venture, including some dramatically changed lives. In the end, however, in crass terms, the return was no longer justifying the investment.

So we canceled the service. The decision not to continue the Saturday night worship was seen by a few as admission of defeat. Yet I believe that decision earned our church leadership the confidence of some people for whom change doesn't come easily. Perhaps that decision established some credibility that will come in handy the next time I or other church leaders make what seems like a radical proposal. Maybe the next time our church launches into a new and unusual program, those who are hesitant to embrace change will think: *Well, if this doesn't work, the leaders will admit it and not be stubborn about it.*

Section Two
THIS AIN'T EASY

But he said to me, "My grace is sufficient for you, for my power is made perfect in weakness." Therefore I will boast all the more gladly about my weaknesses, so that Christ's power may rest on me. That is why, for Christ's sake, I delight in weaknesses, in insults, in hardships, in persecutions, in difficulties. For when I am weak, then I am strong.
—2 Corinthians 12:9–10

6

Battle Scars

Not long ago the National Association of Sports Officials (NASO) published some of the "poor sporting behavior incidents" that had been reported to them. It was almost enough to make me hire a bodyguard when I officiate. Check out a few of the incidents:

North Carolina—Leaders of a recreational basketball league place a "lifetime ban" on the mother of a 14-year-old player after she jumps on the back of an official, scratching his face and the back of his neck.

Oklahoma—A 15-year-old tee-ball umpire was allegedly choked and punched by a 37-year-old assistant coach of a tee-ball team for five- and six-year-olds.

Maryland—According to Hyattsville police, a man has been charged with attempted first-degree murder for an attack on a soccer referee...Doctors informed police that had the knife been slightly longer, the victim would not have survived.

Florida—A coed softball game turned violent when 34-year-old Charles J. Mitchell (Boca Raton) allegedly assaulted and battered 74-year-old volunteer umpire Les Barr during a recreational game in Coconut Creek, Fla.

Stories like these (and there are countless stories like these) have prompted legislators in a number of states to consider new laws intended to crack down on attacks against sports officials.

In fairness, I suppose I should include this incident noted by *Sports Illustrated* a few years back: *Johannesburg (Reuters)— A South African soccer referee pulled a gun and shot dead a coach who questioned one of his rulings, police said on Sunday.*

OK, so officials aren't completely guiltless, but attacks on officials are a lot more common than referees shooting coaches.

Bruised Shins and Skinned Knees

I love speaking with officials who have been at it for a long time. No experienced official is without his or her war stories. When veteran officials get together horror stories abound: threats by parents; being escorted off the field by policemen for protection; and being badgered and berated by coaches and fans.

NASO is reporting a serious shortage of officials. Some have called it a recruiting crisis. According to NASO, the primary reason officials hang up their whistles is bad (sometimes outrageous) behavior from players, coaches, parents, and fans. When surveyed, officials who chose not to come back for a new season responded overwhelmingly that their primary reason was poor sportsmanship by those on the field and in the stands. The abuse leaves many so jaded that they walk away.

Leadership has left a lot of people jaded, too. Innumerable leaders have walked away from their roles. They have decided leadership is not worth the personal cost.

Leadership certainly comes with its great joys, its recognition, and even its perks. There is nothing quite like being at the point of a movement that is accomplishing a meaningful mission. Leadership offers an incomparable sense of meaning and purpose—that one's life really is making a difference.

But make no mistake; leadership does not come without cost. No good leader is so confident and composed that he or she can absorb disparaging remarks, or watch people leave the organization in protest, without feeling some pain. We talk a lot about developing thick skin; and thick skin is necessary. Yet, no matter how well I understand the psychology of conflict, and no matter how well I steel myself against attacks, it still smarts when people slam me. In my case, disapproval is far less devastating than it used to be, but it still stings. Rare is the leader who is immune to the pain of severe criticism.

In *Leadership Jazz*, Max De Pree writes:

If you raise children or grandchildren, you know that by the end of August, they've been running around all summer in their shorts, sneakers, and T-shirts. You also know that their knees and their elbows are always skinned, their shins always black and blue, and that they have the

> *marks of the summer's fracases on their faces. A six year*
> *old boy at the end of August is my picture of a leader.*

De Pree says if you've been leading for a while you're going to have "bruised shins and skinned knees." It seems appropriate, then, simply to acknowledge the difficulties of leadership. If you're up to your eyeballs in alligators, you need to know that you are not alone. "Misery loves company," they say, and if you're in a tough spot as a leader you've got loads of company. If you are considering accepting a leadership position, then be realistic about what you will face. War stories, bruises, and scars come with the territory.

A Lot Is Riding on Your Leadership

In a ball game, bragging rights are at stake. Players know their girlfriends are watching. Coaches know their athletic directors are watching. Win/loss records and championship hopes are on the line. Sure, it's just a game, but people have a lot riding on that game. Adrenaline is pumping. The clock is running. Coaches, players, and officials are making split-second decisions. It is a high-energy, high-anxiety situation. Therefore, it is not surprising that players, fans, and coaches are going to react negatively to some calls. The verbal abuse that officials sometimes suffer is not justifiable, but it also is not altogether shocking.

Likewise, when you lead, a lot is on the line. Employees' ideas of what the organization ought to look like, members' long-held beliefs about the way the organization ought to function, and everybody's comfort zones are at stake. In some cases, careers might even be threatened. Therefore, it is not surprising that people often react very negatively to a leader's decisions.

Difficult leadership—leadership in trying times—demands that we help people look at the world differently. And most folks do not acquire a new worldview without a great deal of discomfort. Change is viewed by many as *loss*, and whether the loss is of a ball game or of one's dreams, people don't take loss easily. Leaders often have to step forth in situations in which the level of angst is high. Thus leaders who make tough calls—even the nice guys—sometimes end up having to pull arrows out of their hide.

Just for Vocational Ministers

When pastors get together, painful stories often arise. I've heard pastors tell about church members who slashed their tires; other ministers tell how their reputations were trashed by folks who knew better. I've heard pastors lament the tears of their spouses and the mind-boggling rancor of their churches. Of course, mistreatment is not limited to pastors. Any role of leadership in the Christian community attracts attacks. The Christian movement has lost many good leaders because of the unfathomable pain inflicted on them by fellow believers. Spiritual leadership can be a costly calling.

Those on the outside of a church, or even those on its periphery, might imagine that leading a church is easy. After all, everyone at church is nice and on the same page, right? Church leaders reading this are probably smiling at just how naive that perception is.

The Lord of the church is perfect; the people of the church are not. War stories, bruises, and scars come with church leadership. And I think wounds inflicted by the church hurt worse and scar more deeply, for we expect more from Christians.

The fact that there is a growing shortage of both pastors and sports officials is not surprising. I hear enough from people who sense a divine call to vocational ministry, and from seminary teachers, to know that intrachurch conflicts are driving people away from the pastorate. There are just too many horror stories. A major reason why spiritual leaders of various roles (not just pastors) give up the mantle of church leadership is that they have been worn down by rancor within the Christian community.

Not only have large numbers of spiritual leaders *abandoned* the church over the wars, bruises, and scars; we now have scores of potential leaders *avoiding* the church for the same reason. Potential leaders know so many mentors, friends, and parents who have been burned by unchristian behavior that these up-and-comers do not want to join the staff of an existing church.

Just this week a seminary administrator told me that one reason so few ministerial students want to *serve in* the local church is because so many ministerial students *grew up in* the local church! They've seen too many pastors and other church staff members roughed up and run off, and they want no part of that. These ministerial students are preparing to serve in parachurch organizations, counseling ministry, chaplaincy, and even new church starts, but existing churches seem too much like a mine field. Even those who plan to join a church staff are particularly hesitant about becoming a senior pastor, since the winds of most church storms eventually shift toward the senior pastor's desk.

None of this makes our job any easier. Nevertheless, perhaps those of you who at this very moment are in the middle of an ecclesiastical storm will find some comfort in the fact that you are not alone. It does come with the territory.

7

This Ain't Easy

One of the most talked-about officiating blunders of the last few years occurred on September 16, 2006, in a college football game between the Oklahoma Sooners and the Oregon Ducks. Oregon, trailing by six points with just over a minute left in the game, attempted an on-side kick. A big-time mêlée ensued at the middle of the field as players in green and players in white battled for the pigskin. At the whistle, the officiating crew signaled Oregon's ball. Oregon would have a chance to win the game with a touchdown and extra point.

But wait.

TV replays showed clearly that an Oregon player touched the ball before it traveled the required ten yards. The ball should have been given to Oklahoma at that spot. What fans watching on TV didn't know was that the official in the booth was not seeing all that they were seeing; on his monitor he could see only one angle from the cameras. The only video feed (view of the play) sent to him was from the end zone, and he did not have conclusive evidence that an Oregon player had touched the ball before it rolled ten yards. Therefore, he did not change the ruling, although just about everybody else could see that his partners down below had missed the call.

That, however, wasn't the worst part. The ruling on the field was that Oregon had recovered the football. Replays showed clearly that Oklahoma's Allen Patrick had possession of the ball when the play ended. So, again, it should have been ruled Oklahoma's ball. Oklahoma then would have had a chance to run out the clock and win the game. Yet the ball was given to Oregon, and the Ducks went on to score and defeat the Sooners.

I feel badly for the officiating crew, for I'm certain they called it as they saw it. Nonetheless, they botched two critical calls on one potentially game-deciding play. The mistakes were honest, but costly. The PAC-10 conference suspended the entire crew for one game. PAC-10 commissioner Tom Hansen even apologized to the University of Oklahoma for the obvious errors.

Harder than It Looks

College and NFL officials truly are my heroes, but even they blow calls once in a while. Officiating is simply harder than it looks. So is leadership. A lot of people think leadership is all about enjoying the limelight, but leadership is tough. The Bible says, "Cast all your anxiety on him because he cares for you" (1 Peter 5:7). It is noteworthy that those words were written in the context of leadership. Leading isn't for cowards. No one ever led in the transformation of a company, or saw a dying organization do a U-turn, or started a business without experiencing some pain along the way. Knowing up front that there will be pain helps take the edge off the anguish of leadership.

A friend of mine leads a complex organization. When he assumed leadership, the organization had been in need of changes for a long time. He courageously took on the task of turning the ship. In doing so, he riled a lot of folks.

I thought of him when I was thumbing through an old *Successories* catalog and saw a painting of a ship in a storm. The caption read, "It doesn't matter who is at the helm of the ship when the seas are calm." I cut out that picture and mailed it to him.

The adage under that painting reminds me that the test of true leadership often comes in the form of a tempest. In fact, in *Managing the Non-Profit Organization*, Peter Drucker gives the following title to one of the chapters: "Leadership is a Foul-Weather Job." There he states, "The one predictable thing in any organization is the crisis. That always comes. That's when you *do* depend on the leader."

Many leaders in both secular and spiritual organizations will be able to identify with Barbara Brown Taylor's story in *The Preaching Life* about the pastor of the Methodist church where she grew up. She loved that pastor, for, although she was just a little girl, he made her feel important. She loved hearing him teach, and his teaching always inspired her to learn more on her own. Then came that awful day:

> *At first all I knew was that something was wrong. Threat hung in the air . . . "Civil rights" had come to Ohio, a phrase*

that made adults talk loudly and lose their tempers. They chose sides and defended them; they wanted my friend (the pastor) to choose sides too, and he did. The doors of the church were open, he said. He would stand there to make sure they remained open, he said, so that is where they hung him—in effigy—a grotesque stuffed figure that bore no resemblance to my friend, swaying in the heat as he packed and left town.

That was when I began to understand that God's call was not only wonderful but also terrible…It had sharp edges to it. It was capable of cutting deep, and those who reached out to grasp it had best be prepared to bleed.

Perhaps you are bleeding now. God's call to leadership—no matter the setting—often has a sharp edge to it. Spiritual leadership is both wonderful and terrible.

Jesus said, "The good shepherd lays down his life for the sheep" (John 10:11). While I don't expect to have to offer my life as a sacrifice for leadership, the truth is that leadership often is costly. This leadership gig ain't as easy as it looks.

Just for Vocational Ministers

The late Earl Strom spent more than 30 years officiating in the NBA and was regarded by many as one of the best referees ever. He described the following incident in *Calling the Shots*: During game four of the 1987 NBA finals, Strom had a microphone on him. The tension had

---

been high for a while, and in the fourth quarter there was a particularly volatile moment between Kevin McHale of the Celtics and Mychal Thompson of the Lakers. Strom was growing impatient with the carping and pushing. The microphone picked up Strom's words: "I should have been a priest."

What made Strom think being a vocational minister would be less stressful than being an NBA referee? In *Leadership That Works*, I found these challenging words from Peter Drucker, who at the time was speaking to a group of senior ministers from large churches:

> *Other than president of the United States, the most difficult jobs in America today are president of a large university, administrator of a large general hospital, and pastor of a large church . . . Pastors are expected to be biblical and theological scholars, business administrators, counselors, public speakers, fund-raisers, and visionaries, plus lead a personal life that is consistent with the values of the church.*

I believe with all my heart that vocational ministry is a blessing. But, as many of you reading this book could testify, that blessing can come with some pretty sharp edges.

8

Change
Is Painful

Have you ever heard of Charlie Finley? From 1960 to 1980 he was the colorful and controversial owner of the American League baseball team, the Athletics, first of Kansas City and later of Oakland. Charlie was the one who thought orange baseballs would be a great idea. He was convinced that players could see and field an orange ball better and that fans could follow it better. The American League actually agreed to an experiment with orange balls in two spring training games in 1973. After the experiment, the orange balls went the way of several other Finley ideas: putting players in white cleats; reducing a walk to three balls and a strike-out to two strikes; promoting Charlie-O the mascot mule; and developing a mechanical contraption ("rabbit") that would pop up from behind home plate and present the ball to the umpire.

Change doesn't come easily to baseball. In fact, I can't think of anywhere that change comes easily. Change, however, is necessary, for if organizations don't change, they die. We must change; but change is dangerous.

The Goldfish Principle

My wife and I once bought our kids a goldfish. A few days later I looked across the room at a fishbowl of murky water and decided to do something nice for my finned friend. I scooped the fish out with my wife's strainer (I knew she wouldn't mind), and put him in a glass of water for holding purposes. Then I poured the cloudy water out of the bowl, washed the bowl, filled the bowl with fresh tap water, and plopped my wet pet into that new water. I thought, *If he could talk, he'd thank me for this.*

I left home to pick up the kids and came back about three hours later and . . . the fish . . . well, let's just say God had called him home. The next day my wife went to buy a more hearty fish. She told the pet store owner what had happened, and he explained what was behind the fish's demise. Alas! He did not die of natural causes.

He died from the sudden change. The expert explained that I should have left the water out for a day or so, then transferred the fish gently to his new home. Sudden change apparently is very traumatic for goldfish.

But before you think too badly of me, consider what would have happened had I *not* changed the water. The poor little fellow would have died a slow, agonizing, suffocating death. Abrupt change is deadly for goldfish. But so is the absence of change.

The same is true for human organizations. Swift change can be traumatic for us. But so is change's absence. Jesus reminded us that you can't pour new wine into old wineskins.

To strike the proper balance as a leader requires courage. When the revolutionaries would kill the fish with traumatic change, the leader must have the courage to say no to some changes. At other times, when staunch traditionalists apparently would prefer the poor fish die a slow, suffocating death, the leader needs courage to change the water.

This is a new day. And in the future, days are going to get newer faster than ever before! In the words of Yogi Berra, "The future ain't what it used to be." Change is not negotiable.

Change is difficult and should not be embarked upon impulsively; but change is necessary, and should not be opposed stubbornly. We must hold in tension those two truths. If we either initiate change without sensitivity to tradition, or oppose change for the mere sake of tradition, we will jeopardize the health of the organization in question. (By the way, I think more fish have died from murky water than from change.)

Ready for Change?

There are three kinds of people in your organization:

- *The folks for whom change—just about any change— seems wonderful.*
- *The folks who are not going to like any change.*
- *The folks who aren't quite sure about change.*

It is among this third group that you will exercise your leadership. The first will follow you just because you're doing something new. The second are not likely to follow no matter how inspirational you are. (The best you can hope for from the second group is permission, and if you get that, then thank God that at least they are willing not to block your initiative.)

In *Leadership Jazz*, Max De Pree outlines some issues to address when considering change. His work stimulated my thinking, and I believe it would be helpful to give you a checklist to help you think through your own proposals. So, as you consider how you will lead the third group—those who aren't sure about the change you are initiating—ask yourself these questions to assess whether or not your organization is ready for something new:

1. Can we *try* it? Is anything keeping us from giving it a test run and an objective evaluation at a certain time? Reluctant people may accept change more easily if they know there is an exit strategy in case it doesn't work. If you are committed to an objective evaluation of your proposed change, and if you are willing to admit it if your idea doesn't work out, then tell that to your organization. You might just give folks the incentive to let you try your new initiative.

2. Does everyone who should have a voice have it? Unwavering convictions are important. But it is also important that people within your organization see that you can handle suggestions and constructive criticism with poise. Reasonable people will accept decisions with which they disagree, as long as the process was a fair one and they believe they were heard.

3. Are we letting people grieve their loss? Acknowledge that the change you are asking people to make is going to result in a loss for them. They are going to have to give up something, whether big or small. It might be a petty habit or a long-held conviction. In any case, trivializing people's losses is poor leadership.

4. How's my heart? There is a difference between destructive change and constructive change. Constructive change occurs when leaders balance passion and vision with servanthood. Destructive change often is a reflection of a leader's cavalier obsession with his or her personal agenda.

Arrogant leadership is simply wrong. Furthermore, it is usually ineffective; people hesitate to follow tyrants. *Farsightedness*, combined with *warmheartedness* and *levelheadedness*, makes change more palatable to everyone. But *farsightedness*, combined with *coldheartedness* and *hotheadedness* in the leader, makes for *coldfeetedness* among the followers.

5. Am I willing for people to leave the organization? And if they leave, how devastating will it be? I don't suggest that we ignore political realities. We have to be prudent, but we must not be constrained by fear. If we have done our homework and prayed and done all within our power to make a good decision, then we must be willing for people to leave.

6. Am I willing to stay? Don't initiate a significant change unless you are planning on staying around for a while. It would be terribly unfair to encourage a group of people to bite off a big chunk of a major project and then not hang around to help them chew it.

7. Have we created a desire for change? An effective way to introduce change is to create tension—a sense of urgency. Help people see the gap between the way things are and the way things could and should be.

8. Are we approaching change overload? An organization can withstand only so much change before it either shuts down—resisting any change—or implodes.

9. Am I, as the leader, willing to take the heat from those who don't like the change? Anticipate potential criticism, and prepare yourself mentally, emotionally and spiritually for it.

10. What are influential people in the organization saying about this change? Some people have earned the right to have their opinions weighed more heavily than others. And, frankly, knowing the opinions of the influencers in your organization (whether or not they deserve that influence) is just prudent leadership. Is there an effective alliance of key people who are committed to change?

11. Is this change just a pet project for me or will it actually facilitate the fulfillment of our mission? Some of us who enjoy leadership get an adrenaline rush out of change. For most folks, change is tough. I can't afford to put others through the pain of change just so I can get my kicks.

12. Is there a reasonable likelihood that eventually this change will be seen as a successful move? I'm not encouraging timidity. Great things are never accomplished without risk. Nevertheless, it is best to wait until you sense a realistic shot at success.

13. Have I communicated the vision sufficiently?
If the organization is not tired of hearing the vision, the answer to this question probably is no.

14. Am I willing to make significant sacrifices to see this through?
There will be criticisms and unanticipated obstacles. If I'm not willing to suffer through some tough days, then it's not fair to the organization for me to initiate this change.

Honestly wrestling with these questions will prepare you to embark on the daring adventure of leading your organization through change.

Just for Vocational Ministers

In *Empowering Your Church Through Creativity and Change*, David Goetz writes:

> *Making changes at church is a little like kicking a sleeping grizzly. Or playing with her cubs. You risk getting mauled.*
>
> *People say they want change and improvement, but I've never heard a layperson say, "I love our pastor because he is so creative and makes so many wonderful changes."*

And I'd venture to say most Christian organizations are nearly as hesitant to change as local churches are. Yet churches and other Christian organizations are no less in need of change than are other bodies. Change is difficult, but change is necessary.

In addition to the questions listed above, I would add one more: "Can we change by addition, not subtraction?" If something is no longer contributing to the mission of the organization, there should be no question about discarding it. However, assuming there is some benefit from the present practice, change by addition (adding another effective practice) is less disruptive to the church. For example, adding a worship service is usually more helpful than replacing a present worship service with another one.

SECTION THREE
POISE

Since an overseer is entrusted with God's work, he must be blameless—not overbearing, not quick-tempered, not given to drunkenness, not violent, not pursuing dishonest gain. Rather he must be hospitable, one who loves what is good, who is self-controlled, upright, holy and disciplined.
—Titus 1:7–8

9

Poise Means...

The basketball game is tied with the clock running out. Bragging rights and championship hopes hang in the balance. The atmosphere is electric. The tension is so thick you can cut it with a knife. The coaches' faces are red. The fans are screaming. The players on the bench are not on the bench.

And then there are the officials. From the looks on their faces you'd think the game is in the first half with one team ahead by 30 points. They are cool. Calm. Collected. They have the untroubled demeanor of folks who know the rules and know themselves. They look as if their blood pressure is the same as it was when they were sipping coffee and reading the newspaper this morning.

OK, it's not always like that. But it's true of the really good officials. They are *under* control and *in* control. They are alert and focused, but uninvolved emotionally. They are poised.

Major League Baseball (MLB) umpires could be called exceptions, I guess. They sometimes engage in nose-to-nose shouting matches that you'd never see in other sports. By and large, however, sports officials keep their cool and keep their distance from irate coaches.

What Poise Is and Is Not

If I go to a ball game as a fan, I love to watch the officials. When the players, coaches, and spectators are in a tizzy, I keep my eye on the refs. Usually their faces are as calm as a placid pool.

Occasionally, in a tense meeting, I'll watch the leader like I watch basketball officials. Some people in the room are spoiling for a fight. Others are afraid of a fight. But in the face of the really good leader there is calm. He or she is unruffled and relaxed. His or her blood may be boiling, but his or her demeanor is reassuringly tranquil. There is something about the leader's composure that says to the pugnacious ones, "You aren't going to bully me," and to the frightened ones, "Everything is going to be all right."

I pray for that kind of strength. I want to be that kind of leader. I want to be poised.

I'm not talking, of course, about adhering to the hollow leadership philosophy of "Never let 'em see you sweat." I'm talking about genuine calm—what, in the world of athletics, might be called "mental toughness."

I'm not talking about those leaders who are so naïve that they're the last to know the organization is in trouble. I'm talking about emulating leaders who recognize the seriousness of a grave situation yet do not panic.

I'm also not talking about keeping a poker-faced, deadpan expression. There's nothing wrong with the group seeing the leader's passions. A little animation from the one in charge never hurt anybody. It's OK to vigorously defend a position;

it's not OK to turn red and say something stupid. I'm talking about genuine poise.

- Poise means *responding* to crises; not *reacting* to crises.
- Poise means choosing not to say something you're going to regret later.
- Poise means maintaining objectivity and composure, though the pressure has gotten so intense nobody would blame you for a wild outburst.
- Poise means being gracious toward your critics, when nobody would be surprised if you were to choke them.
- Poise means being willing to make the tough call, though everyone knows that, down deep, you are scared.
- Poise means maintaining your dignity when throwing an old-fashioned fit is tempting.
- Poise is keeping your cool without being aloof or arrogant.
- Poise is refusing to be petty and refusing to hold someone's past behavior against them.
- Poise is serenity—a refusal to be provoked.

Let's look deeper at some of the traits and actions of the poised leader.

A Gentle Leader

The poised leader is careful in how he or she responds to critics. There are words that officials can say that escalate conflict. *Shut up and sit down!*, for example, is not going to ease tensions between the official and the coach. Nor is, *Why don't you coach and let me officiate?!* While such comments might make the official feel better momentarily, they probably are not going to defuse a volatile situation. And *Read the rule book, Coach!* is probably not going to encourage better study habits on the part of the guy in the official's ear.

There are better ways to speak to an unhappy coach. A simple *That's enough* works well. A matter-of-fact *I've heard enough* is effective. When the official says, with calm confidence, *That's not the way I saw it, Coach,* it's hard for the coach to argue further. When a coach crosses the line, Steve Shaw, a Southeastern Conference (SEC) football official, likes to say, "Coach, do you care to repeat that?"

I was officiating an important game recently when I witnessed a foul but reacted too slowly and didn't throw the flag. Coaches screamed bloody murder. After the play ended I acknowledged, "Coach, I missed that one." Nobody on that sideline said another word about it.

Proverbs 15:1 reads, "A gentle answer turns away wrath." Of course neither officials nor other leaders can afford to be weak, but there is a big difference between weakness and gentle answers. Gentle answers come from one who is well-prepared and confident. Gentle answers grow out of a strong character, not out of weakness. Christian gentleness says: *I have the ability to lash out. That's my choice and no one can take it away from me. But I will choose not to. I will choose the way of Jesus, the way of gentleness.*

Not long after I arrived to teach at the seminary in Ogbomoso, Nigeria, I reacted fairly harshly a couple of times to my students. My abrasiveness partially stemmed from my insecurity with living in a new country and working at a new job. Yet, no matter the cause, I had responded unkindly, in a curt, stern tone, and louder than was appropriate.

So, I wrote Proverbs 15:1 on a piece of paper as neatly as I could and taped it to the concrete wall of my office. I needed a reminder to give gentle answers, for gentle answers are more Christian than brusque responses. They are also more effective. Gentle answers usually disarm explosive people, whether in a gym, a classroom, or a board meeting.

Confronting Appropriately

My friend John Moreau officiated Division I basketball for 32 seasons. His demeanor is one of his greatest strengths and made him a widely admired official, especially in the highly competitive Atlantic Coast Conference, where he spent 25 years.

He told me about one night when he was officiating at East Carolina University (ECU) and the home team was not playing well. ECU's coach, watching his players perform at a sub-par level, was terribly frustrated, and the officials were bearing the brunt of that frustration. During a time-out, Moreau borrowed a towel from the team manager, walked over in front of East Carolina's coach, and pretended to be wiping up a wet spot on the floor. So that no one other than the coach could hear, Moreau said politely, "Coach, please let us work the game." Then he stood, tossed the towel to the team manager, and play resumed.

After the game, there came a knock on the door of the officials' locker room. A security guard said, "The coach would like to speak with you." The coach stepped out from behind the security guard and said to Moreau, "I just want to say how much I appreciate the way in which you let me know I'd reached my limit."

The moral of that story is that when people reach the limit of propriety, the leader needs to let them know it. But there is a right way and a wrong way to do that. Let's be poised, and communicate in a way that doesn't rob people of their dignity, put them on the offensive, embarrass them, or heighten the tension. After all, Galatians 6:1 reads, "Brothers, if someone is caught in a sin, you who are spiritual should restore him gently."

"Command Presence"

NCAA football official Dan Louie has said, "Coaches are like piranha...They smell blood, they swarm, and they go into a feeding frenzy." Coaches are not alone in that. A lot of folks seem energized when they perceive weakness in the leader. So how do spiritual leaders keep themselves safe from the piranha? Lloyd Rediger suggests the answer is "command presence":

> Command presence . . . is often vital to leadership. Though this is a term I learned in military service, I am not advocating giving orders, macho dominance, or arrogance. . . . I am talking about the often quiet confidence of wisdom and the visible authority of legitimate purpose. . . . This command is apparent as physical posture, in direct eye contact, in nondefensiveness, in speaking with disciplined authority. Command presence

says, "I know what I am doing" and "Don't mess with
me!".... This representative, commanding presence
is a natural development of a healthy body, mind, and
spirit. It is not an ego trip or a manipulative performance.
When you see it, you know it.
—Clergy Killers

Poise truly is something that you just know when you see it. And that kind of poise does minimize conflict, because antagonists think twice before assailing someone who has the command presence that poise gives to a leader.

Command presence, I believe, can be practiced and learned. In *Psychology of Officiating*, Weinberg and Richardson write, "Because your thoughts, feelings, and behaviors are interrelated, the more you act confidently, the more likely you will be to feel confident...Project an appearance of confidence, and your doubt will disappear." While poise ultimately comes from within, a confident exterior will help gain the respect you deserve.

"Emotional Intelligence"

Daniel Goleman has done a great service for leaders by researching and writing about "emotional intelligence." From reading Goleman's works, especially *Emotional Intelligence* and *Working with Emotional Intelligence*, I've learned some really interesting things about our brains. When we experience an external stimulus—when we see, touch, smell, taste, or hear something—that stimulus rushes to two parts of our brains: our emotional brain, the amygdala, and the rational brain, the neocortex. The problem is that there is a shortcut to the

TOUGH CALLS

emotional brain, so a few milliseconds before we are able to *think* about something, we *feel* something.

That's why, when you are sitting in a room alone, wrapped up in some activity, and someone suddenly appears, you jump like someone just shot electrical current through your chair. Your amygdala signals danger before your neocortex says, *Chill out! It's just Billy from down the hall!* That is called a "precognitive emotion"—a reaction based on bits of sensory information that haven't been sorted through.

All of us have those precognitive emotions. How often have you said, "I reacted before I thought," or, "I must not have been thinking." The biblical meaning of self-control is to get a grip—to get a handle on—our responses and decisions instead of being guided by our flawed emotions and faulty impulses. I guess we could say that poise is learning not to let our amygdalas get us into trouble.

Just for Vocational Ministers

Not many qualities are more essential for the vocational minister than poise. You and I feel passionately about what we do, and when we feel like church members are impeding progress or being myopic, we get fired up. It's one thing to lead with enthusiasm, but it's a small step from enthusiasm to unbridled emotion. If we aren't careful, passion will trump prudence. We could end up saying things we later regret, or becoming so impassioned that we lose our objectivity. A lack of poise can even cost us our ministry.

10

Under Control

Control of the game begins with the official. When an official loses control of himself, he gives implicit permission to the coaches and players to lose control as well. Dan Louie is an NCAA football official and often leads training sessions for other officials. In his workshop "What Makes an Excellent Official," Louie declares, "This is an emotional game and we must keep our emotions in check at all times.... This is the best compliment we can give to an official we are observing.... to say that he looked poised and in control."

Leaders, too, must maintain an inner calm in the face of hostility, both for their own sake and for the sake of their leadership.

What Poised Leaders Do

- **Poised leaders calm the storm.** Daniel Goleman, in *Emotional Intelligence*, discusses what he calls "emotional contagion." His premise is that if we convey calm, then that calm is going to be contagious. He also uses the term *emotional entrainment*, which is the ability to shape others' emotions by conveying our own. (Influence, by the way, is the shorthand definition of leadership.) So, if Goleman is right, we lead—influence others—through emotional entrainment. If we display confidence when everyone else is panicking, and if we radiate charity when everyone else is fighting, then we are leading. So if you want to be a leader, learn to keep your cool. Cool is contagious and influential.

• **Poised leaders defuse volatile situations.** There is no place for belligerence in spiritual leadership. If you take delight in controversy—if you secretly enjoy a good scrap—then you are not a spiritual leader. When it's time to stand for what's right, a spiritual leader can mix it up with the best of them. A truly spiritual leader, however, is always going to be seeking ways to de-escalate a volatile situation. He or she will not sacrifice the mission of the organization on the altar of peace, yet Jesus's last prayer—the prayer for the unity of His followers—is always at the back of the spiritual leader's mind. Effective leaders keep their composure, coolly evaluate conflict, and defuse hostilities.

• **Poised leaders act as the organization's ballasts and shock absorbers.** The leader can serve the organization well by willingly absorbing the indignation of a few disgruntled people. It's like the old saying, "If they're talking about me they're giving someone else a break." If the leader can withstand being the focus of complaints, then the rest of the organization is being spared. (Of course, this holds true only to a point, because excessive attacks on the leader ultimately hurt the health of the entire organization.)

Furthermore, the leader is like a ballast—the counterweight that keeps a ship balanced even in a storm. A calm, poised, strong leader provides stability. Even though the ship may rock, no one will worry about the ship tipping over if the leader is composed and secure.

Calm in the Storm

In the previous chapter, I mentioned my friend John Moreau as an experienced official with a reassuring demeanor. Video from a game he officiated between the University of California Los Angeles (UCLA) and Michigan shows him at his best.

It was the second round of the 1993 West Regional in the NCAA men's basketball tournament. UCLA's coach Jim Harrick and Michigan's coach Steve Fisher. March Madness.

The game went into overtime. No. 1 seed Michigan finally scored to go ahead 86-84 with less than two seconds left in the game. The arena erupted. Michigan would advance to the Sweet 16.

But hang on.

Had Jalen Rose's attempt beaten the shot clock? Several tense minutes passed while the officials talked things over with the guys at the scorer's table. Coaches Fisher and Harrick vociferously voiced their opinions. Commentators Digger Phelps and Greg Gumbel tried to narrate the confusion for those watching on TV, and were not completely complimentary of the officiating crew's handling of the situation. John Moreau, along with his partners, Don Rutledge and Andre Pattitto, were trying to untangle the imbroglio.

Above the noise on the video you can hear Moreau declaring, "Everything's gonna be all right." It would be stretching it to say his words calmed the storm like Jesus's "Peace, be still." But the officials did eventually come to a conclusion—Jimmy King's put-back basket off Jalen Rose's shot counted—and Michigan advanced to the next round.

Moreau's declaration is an example of poised leadership. It is always reassuring (especially to those who are not at the center of the conflict) to hear someone with authority say, "Everything's gonna be all right."

Just for Vocational Ministers

Pastor Rene Schlaepfer of Twin Lakes Church, Aptos, California, tells a story that illustrates the power of poise:

I saw this in the first church I served as youth pastor. The board had fired a beloved staff member. At the next congregational meeting, a shouting match erupted— and it was suddenly all about the senior pastor. "You're boring!" they shouted. Totally out of control.

The pastor and his wife took it. They never stopped being calm and Christ-like through the whole thing. The church split in half in that one meeting. I eventually decided I'd rather follow a godly, serene man than a live wire who doesn't display the fruit of the Spirit.
—"Keeping Conflict Healthy," *Leadership*, Fall 2004

Chalk up another one for poise.

11

The Roots
of Poise

Poise comes more naturally for some, for temperament is largely innate. Yet all of us can learn to become increasingly poised. One's disposition is not set in proverbial stone. The brain, to a degree, is malleable; it matures and adjusts when we ask it to do so.

Poise can be learned. Certainly some of us inherited a shorter fuse than others, but we can learn to control our fuses. We can indeed learn to keep our amygdalas in check until our neocortexes have time to assess things. We can learn to prevent our adrenal glands from ruining our lives. We can train our brains.

Of course a key to learning poise is to understand its sources. Legendary UCLA basketball coach John Wooden writes:

I define poise as being true to oneself, not getting rattled, thrown off, or unbalanced regardless of the circumstances or situation. This may sound easy, but Poise can be a most elusive quality in challenging times. Leaders lacking

Poise panic under pressure. Poise means holding fast to your beliefs and acting in accordance with them, regardless of how bad or good the situation may be . . . Poise means having a brave heart in all circumstances . . . Few characteristics are more valuable to a leader than Poise, especially when she or he is under pressure. And that's what leaders are paid to do, perform under pressure.
—*Wooden on Leadership*, with Steve Jamison

Wooden goes on to say that we don't acquire poise; poise *acquires us* when we have been disciplined enough to develop a strong character. Specifically, Wooden believes poise "arrives unexpectedly and without fanfare" if we follow right practices.

Does a leader just decide to be poised? Well, in a sense, yes. Poise is largely a choice. But it is not quite that simple. Wooden is right; poise grows out of right practices and strong character traits.

Getting to the Roots

- **Poise is rooted in spiritual disciplines.** The person who is connected with God, by faith, through Jesus, has a potential that is unique. The presence and power of God's Spirit in our lives gives us the ability to be poised persons. Furthermore, we can connect with the Father in the same way that Jesus did, through spiritual disciplines, and become increasingly poised.

Some sage quipped, "Life is like a tube of toothpaste. You never know what's inside until you're squeezed." So when *you* get squeezed, what comes out? If bitter words and a caustic tone emerge, then something is wrong inside.

Therefore, nurture your spirit. Make corporate worship your lifestyle, not just a hit or miss activity. Get up early and read your Bible and pray. When those big decisions and events come along, go on a 24-hour fast. Join a small group and/or a Bible study class of your peers. Get some Christian music CDs and make drive time spiritual renewal time. Nurture your spirit. And your spirit will become more poised.

Jesus said, "I am the vine; you are the branches. If a man remains in me and I in him, he will bear much fruit; apart from me you can do nothing" (John 15:5).

• **Poise is rooted in self-differentiation.** *Self-differentiation* is a term borrowed from biology. It describes cells that cooperate, but, as individual cells, they are self-sufficient. People who understand biology a lot better than I do explain that these individual cells do not isolate themselves; yet they understand their self-determination, their individuality.

Likewise, self-differentiated leaders are those who function within a system (i.e., an organization) but whose sense of value and well-being is not dependent upon that system. Because they don't believe their worth is derived from the system, they are not threatened by stresses within the system. They don't see criticisms as personal attacks, and they can respond objectively.

Self-differentiated people can practice a non-anxious presence, even when their position on an issue is under attack by others. Their sense of worth comes from inside, and thus is not threatened by an external conflict. It is not that these people are aloof, but they do have a sense of calm that defies the relational storms brewing around them.

• **Poise is rooted in self-control.** The New Testament speaks often of the need for self-control. The Greek word translated into English as "self-control" in Galatians 5:23 is *egkrateia*, which literally means "holding oneself in." A closely related word, translated "self-control" in Titus 2, is *sophronismos*. *Sophronismos* comes from a root word meaning "to grip" or "to take hold of."

The biblical meaning of self-control, then, is "getting a grip," taking hold of our responses to stressful stimuli. Those two Greek words for self-control (*egkrateia* and *sophronismos*) actually encompass the nuances of a number of English words: self-discipline, self-control, good sense, moderation, prudence, sober-mindedness, and sound mind.

So to practice biblical self-control is to get a grip on ourselves, to think clearly and act responsibly, even when the heat or the pressure is on. It means to use good judgment, to think about the likely consequences of what we are about to say or do, even in highly charged situations. Self-control is not the suppressing of emotions, but rather the appropriate expression of emotions.

Let's return for a moment to Goleman's work on *Emotional Intelligence*. It is the amygdala that triggers our emotional response even before we have had time to think about the new stimulus. We do not have the ability to circumvent the amygdala, short of having it removed. (And brain surgery seems a bit radical.) What we *can* do is learn better to control how long that emotional response will last. We can learn to cool our jets, and thus respond constructively. We can learn self-control.

Self-control is far, far more than learning to say no. Self-control grows out of a deep, compelling awareness of what's important. We often think of self-control only in terms of denying ourselves something that might be bad for us but sure would be a lot of fun. Self-control often seems like nothing more than clenching our teeth—grinning and bearing our way through life—and then pitying ourselves for missing out on so much good stuff.

Self-control certainly does include self-denial, but it is more about priorities. Self-control is choosing what is best over the rest. Following Stephen Covey's line of thinking in *First Things First*, I believe self-control can be described as regarding some things as so important that we won't sacrifice them for fleeting and insignificant pleasures. Saying "yes" to what we value allows us to say "no" to what is less important. Our families, our congregations, our futures, our integrity, and our spiritual health are all too valuable to jeopardize for the sake of things that might seem momentarily enticing but are actually of little worth.

The health and mission of the organization or community in which we serve; self-respect; personal goals and dreams— all these contribute to the yes that should allow us to say no to anything that conflicts with our values and principles, including the temptation to slap that knucklehead who seems intent on making us miserable.

• **Poise is rooted in self-esteem.** Weinberg and Richardson write in *Psychology of Officiating*:

> You need a strong sense of self and a high level of motivation to overcome the lack of praise and ample criticism you'll receive as an official. You can't be overly concerned about how other people view or evaluate your performance.

I'm convinced that these authors are right; poise is rooted in "a strong sense of self." Why is it that some people always feel the need to have their way? Why do some people lash out at others and feel a need to belittle people? One significant reason is insecurity, a poor self-image, a lack of self-confidence. If we do not feel good about ourselves—if we feel insecure and inferior—then we have a constant need to prove ourselves, to exert our authority, to try to convince ourselves and others that we are of worth. We might throw our weight around in a twisted attempt to cover up for what we feel are inadequacies.

Would you like to be more poised? It might require believing, really believing, the truth that you are of great worth. You have nothing to prove. God shaped you even before you were born. God had you in mind when He brought the cells together that made you. You are of value, not based on how you compare to someone else, but because of your value in the eyes and heart of God. If you will believe that, gentleness will come much more easily.

The Apostle John writes that "Jesus knew that the Father had put all things under his power, and that he had come from God and was returning to God; *so* he got up from the meal, took off his outer clothing, and wrapped a towel around his waist" (John 13:3–4, emphasis added). It was because Jesus understood His Father-given role that He was able to humble Himself and be a servant. Several commentators write that Jesus's understanding of His worth and position in the Father's eyes enabled Him to be emotionally secure enough to wash the disciples' feet. In the *Bible Exposition Commentary*, Warren Wiersbe says it was because Jesus knew who He was, what He had, where He had come from, and where He was going that He could humble Himself.

So let's recognize, as did Jesus, who we are, what we have, where we have come from, and where we are going. Then we can have confidence in our leadership roles. If we are where God placed us, then we should be confident in His wisdom— that He has anointed us, set us aside, for this very life purpose.

Just for Vocational Ministers

Those of us who lead within churches and other Christian communities often have a hard time with poise. That is true for a couple of reasons. One, we tend to be people pleasers, and when someone is unhappy with us our response is not always rational. Second, our identity is so intertwined with our roles that it is very difficult for us to accept criticism of our role performance without believing it to be a personal attack. That is why I always recommend that leaders of Christian organizations study Thomas Fischer, Edwin Friedman, and other writers who address such important issues as self-differentiation. Self-differentiation allows us to appreciate our roles within the church system without becoming dependent upon that system for affirmation. Thus, we can be objective without being aloof, involved without being emotionally dependent. Our churches need that from us.

12

More Roots
of Poise

We are still talking about poise, and that is no accident. There are few qualities more important for sports officials and spiritual leaders than poise, so let's continue to consider the roots of this important leadership attribute.

- **Poise is rooted in self-understanding.** Self-understanding, or self-awareness, means being alert to one's own disposition. It is the ability to stand outside yourself and watch yourself react, analyzing your performance under pressure. The leader who desires to be poised must possess this emotional self-awareness. The ability to recognize the onset of volatile emotions, and to check them before they erupt into inappropriate responses, makes for effective leaders in tough times.

Self-understanding also means being aware of your weaknesses. Leaders ought to learn all they can about themselves, including what their hot buttons are. If I know the issues that set me off, and I understand why those things trigger my emotions, then I am better able to keep my cool in an intense conversation.

Self-understanding requires a basic knowledge of the way God wired us. Our bodies are conditioned to go on high alert when our minds perceive a potential threat. Hormones are released that tighten our muscles, quicken our heart rate, and prepare us to defend ourselves. This fight-or-flight reaction was God's idea, and He gave it to us for our protection. Our brains send signals to the adrenal glands saying, *Get ready for action!*

The problem is that our adrenal glands have a hard time distinguishing between, *A man with a knife is about to attack,* and *This meeting is becoming contentious*. That lack of discernment on the part of the adrenal gland can cause problems, for the appropriate response to an armed mugger and the appropriate response to a tempestuous meeting are very different. While our bodies' physical reaction prepares us well to fend off an attacker, it actually decreases our ability to make prudent decisions and reasonable statements in an impassioned conversation. Levelheadedness is tough when your heart feels like it's going to pound its way out of your chest.

We can't exert complete control over our adrenal glands, but simply being mindful of our body's involuntary reactions can help us remain poised. And we can cultivate self-awareness by: (1) keeping a constant and intentional eye on our emotional thermometer; (2) committing to regular times of meditation during which we reflect on our responses in unpleasant situations; and (3) seeking input from people who love us enough to be candid about how they perceive our reactions under pressure.

- **Poise is rooted in prayer—even a quick prayer.** Do

you remember the time Nehemiah stood before his boss, King Artaxerxes, to make an unusual request? Nehemiah was nervous as he broached the subject of leaving the king's service to go rebuild Jerusalem's walls. Nehemiah 2:4–5 reads: "The king said to me, 'What is it you want?' Then I prayed to the God of heaven, and I answered the king." Nehemiah breathed a prayer before he opened his mouth. When you and I have sweaty palms and wobbly knees, the Creator will gladly answer a heat-of-the-moment request for wisdom and courage.

- **Poise is rooted in self-coaching.** Poise requires self-understanding and a keen awareness of the situation in which you find yourself. Self-coaching is required. Yes, talking to yourself.

There is an example of self-coaching in the Bible. Again we turn to Nehemiah. Many of the wealthy in Jerusalem were taking advantage of hard times to squeeze money out of the poor, and Nehemiah was justifiably angry. As he confronted the nobles and rulers with their sin, he faced a potentially explosive situation.

Nehemiah 5:7 reads, "I consulted with myself and contended with the nobles and the rulers" (NASB). Charles Swindoll notes in *Hand Me Another Brick* that "consulted with myself" can be translated, "to give one self-advice, to counsel one-self." Swindoll writes, "Yes, he [Nehemiah] got mad, but he thought before he spoke. In those moments of self-consultation, God was able to speak to Nehemiah about what to say next." Before Nehemiah lashed out impulsively at the greedy and unethical rich folks, he talked to himself!

I can't say that I am always poised, but when I *am* poised, it is usually because I'm talking myself through the situation.

I am telling myself things like: *This is about the position you are taking; it's not about you, so don't take it personally. Be dispassionate. Respond; don't react. Relax your facial muscles. Take a few deep breaths.*

- **Poise is rooted in experience.** Poise is a skill as well as a character trait. Emotional control can be learned through practice. There are two ways to get that practice. One way is through actually remaining poised during stressful situations—surviving the bona fide battles. The other way to practice poise is through visualization—anticipating what might occur in a tense situation and then thinking through how to respond. Visualization will be discussed below.

Certainly the most effective way to practice poise is simply to survive the difficult challenges of leadership. The most poised sports officials I know are the guys who have spent many a night in the heat of the battle. They have heard every insult fans have to offer. They have made their mistakes and have seen the sun come up the next morning. They have also had their successes and gained confidence from them. They have witnessed the good, the bad, and the ugly of sporting events. They have survived the trenches.

The PhD in poise is earned only in the school of hard knocks. Poise comes through the pain of difficult encounters. Maybe that insight will help us thank God for unpleasant experiences.

- **Poise is rooted in visualization.** Visualization, or imagery, is popular among professional athletes. Sports psychologists help players envision themselves making big plays in pressure-packed situations. Leaders also can use visualization as a tool to help them prepare for those powder-keg-like circumstances that often develop.

You probably know which meetings are going to involve controversy. When you know you are going to face a tough situation, imagine what might happen and what might be said. Then think of how you will respond and how you may answer the charges. Picture the room in which the meeting will take place, and maybe even where you are likely to be sitting. Think about who will speak—you probably already know who will lead the opposition. Think about what they will say. Then imagine yourself responding in a calm and logical manner, no matter how obstreperous others may become. Mentally rehearse the exchanges. Think about your negative tendencies and imagine responding differently than you might have in the past. Picture your facial expression and imagine the tone of your voice.

By rehearsing the scenario in your mind, you prepare yourself to be poised. Ponder the things that might anger or upset you, and then imagine yourself remaining calm in spite of those things. Admit that there are people who have the power to set you off, and picture yourself responding gently to their shenanigans.

Regarding imagery, Weinberg and Richardson in *Psychology of Officiating* write:

> *"Performers establish a mental blueprint for successfully completing the desired action. Thus imagery facilitates performance by blueprinting or coding actions into symbols that make actions more familiar and perhaps more automatic."*

Thus, through visualization you actually prepare your brain

to respond in a certain way to specific circumstances. Just as athletes can condition their bodies to respond in a certain way when they want to shoot, catch, hit, or kick a ball during an intense athletic contest, you can condition your mind to respond in a certain way when you want to say something appropriate during an intense confrontation.

- **Poise is rooted in daily decisions.** Poise is both a gift and a learned practice. Some people are, by nature, less high-strung than others. There are some folks whose pulse never seems to race and whose blood pressure never seems to rise. They are calm, cool, and collected no matter the circumstance. At least they appear to be. It just seems to be their nature.

For most of us, poise is a learned practice. And like anything else, there is a progression in the learning of the skill. Poise in the little things—handling a critical email or an anonymous letter—is a building block to learning how to remain dispassionate when both the heat and the spotlight are on. One can prepare for the inevitable big deal by practicing poise in the little deals. If you can handle a slightly irritated neighbor's phone call, by taking a deep breath and controlling your feelings, you can become the kind of leader who remains calm even when the entire board is on your case.

I must confess that I find this principle easier to preach than to practice, for I am usually more poised professionally than personally. That is, I am more likely to remain calm leading a tense board meeting or officiating a tight football game than I am to keep my cool in the presence of my own family. For example, not so long ago my wife and our 17-year-old son were with me in my old pickup truck when it spat, sputtered, then quit on me in the middle of heavy traffic. My response was, well, not poised.

I am not proud of my words and my actions in that situation. I blew a chance to demonstrate composure in front of my wife and son. I missed an opportunity to prepare for the next high-profile pressure cooker by failing to practice poise in my stalled pickup. I lost out on an opportunity to deepen my character. One day my edginess in a broken down truck might come back to bite me—when I lose my cool in a more public situation.

The depth of character that demonstrates poise in extreme situations is developed over time—through years of doing the little things right. In *The Seven Habits of Highly Effective People*, Stephen R. Covey quotes nineteenth-century clergyman Phillips Brooks:

> *Some day, in the years to come, you will be wrestling with the great temptation or trembling under the great sorrow of your life. But the real struggle is here now . . . Now it is being decided whether, in the day of your supreme sorrow or temptation, you shall miserably fail or gloriously conquer. Character cannot be made except by a steady, long continued process.*

Those words have meant a great deal to me over the years. Every day we make little decisions that shape our characters—little decisions that determine what we will do when the big temptation or crisis comes. It is the private victories in the so-called little battles that enable us to win the big, public battles.

• **Poise is rooted in deep faith.** I used to be a Dallas Cowboys fan. I defected when Jerry Jones bought the team and sacked my hero, the late Coach Tom Landry. When some other coaches were pacing like lions and cursing like sailors and, of all things, abusing the officials—when John Madden had to retire from coaching professional football because of ulcers—Tom Landry was personifying self-control.

How was that? In Michael Zigarelli's *Faith at Work*, Landry is quoted as saying:

> *My relationship with Christ gives me a source of power I would not have otherwise. What eats you up inside is fear and anxiety. God does not give us fear, but power and love and self-control.*

Zigarelli goes on to praise Landry: "Today Tom Landry is renowned not only for his win-loss record, but for being a contemporary role model for workplace Christians everywhere. His legacy is one of both character and success."

Just for Vocational Ministers

If I often find myself getting bent out of shape, I might be mistaking myself for God. If I find myself too stressed out about the way things are going at the church I lead, I might be forgetting that I'm just the undershepherd, not the Head Shepherd.

Knowing that ultimately God is in control does not minimize my responsibility to give my best to His church; it simply reminds me that it is just that—*His* church. I love the way Teresa McBean, one of our ministry staff members, puts it: "There is a God, and you and I didn't get the job." If I'd always remember that, I'd probably be more poised.

SECTION FOUR
CRITICISM AND CONFLICT

Do not repay anyone evil for evil. Be careful to do what is right in the eyes of everybody. If it is possible, as far as it depends on you, live at peace with everyone. Do not take revenge, my friends, but leave room for God's wrath, for it is written: "It is mine to avenge; I will repay," says the Lord.
—Romans 12:17–21

13

Don't Take
It Personally

In his book *You Threw the Flag,* (coauthored with Dan Wilford and C. Stephen Byrum), Ned Wilford tells an enlightening story about the relationship between coaches and officials.

It was the 1990 Blockbuster Bowl matching Penn State versus Florida State, and Wilford was officiating. Wilford had already officiated two big Penn States games in the preceding years—both close and controversial losses to the University of Alabama. In the pregame meeting of coaches, officials, and television representatives, Penn State's Coach Joe Paterno recognized Wilford and engaged him in a warm conversation. The legendary coach admitted he sometimes gets a bit overheated on the sideline and might just be a bit too intense in the way he speaks to officials.

Finally, Paterno put both his hands on Wilford's shoulders and said, "Ned, in spite of what I call you tomorrow, I really do love your mother, your wife, and your kids." The Hall of Fame coach was admitting that he didn't intend for his heat-of-the-game rants to get personal, but unfortunately they might be taken that way.

An Easy Target

It's hard for a leader not to take complaints personally—at least it is for *me*. That's a weakness that I'm trying to overcome. I know in my head that I have to separate the grievance from my identity. I'm getting better at doing that, but I still have to make a conscious decision not to let my emotions and ego get wrapped up in whatever the hullabaloo-of-the-day happens to be.

One of the most important lessons a leader or official can learn is not to take criticism personally. Of course there may be those cases when someone has it in for the leader or official. In most cases, however, the leader is simply the convenient object of someone's displeasure. It is the leader's or official's visibility that makes him or her a target. I remember an older gentleman saying to me once, "It's the chicken that sticks its head up that gets shot at."

In the early 1900s, there was a rule in Major League Baseball that if a fielder was throwing the ball in an attempt to throw out a base runner and the ball hit an umpire, then the runner was automatically out. Of course the smart fielders figured out that it was often easier to hit the umpire than to throw out the runner, so umpires became targets.

Fortunately for umpires, that rule is no longer in the books. Unfortunately for leaders, however, it is often easier for people to fling their indictments at the leader than to address the issue that needs addressing. Don't be surprised if you become a target.

People often need someone to blame. If a team is losing, for example, the officials become convenient targets. It seems culpability has to rest somewhere, and it's hard to blame your teammates or coaches. It's even harder to take the blame yourself. It never has seemed difficult, however, to point the finger at an official.

Likewise, when people are uncomfortable with change, or when they are unhappy with their role, or when the organization is going in a direction with which they are not pleased, *somebody* has to be blamed. That somebody usually is the leader. So don't take it personally.

Furthermore, transference is an issue when it comes to leaders. Sometimes people will transfer the feelings they have toward some significant person in their life to you. And what they transfer might not be positive. You might bear the brunt of someone's resentment toward some other authority figure in his or her life.

Long-time NFL referee Jim Tunney, now retired, puts in perspective:

> *The first time I put on the black-and-white stripes and heard the boos, I wondered, Why are they booing me? I made the right call.*
>
> *I came to realize that the fans were not upset with Jim Tunney. They are partisans, yelling at the authority that has punished them. I happened to be that authority.*
>
> *Sociologists and psychologists tell us that it can be healthy for people to vent their frustrations on something as innocuous as an official making a call in a football game.*

Booing is a vicarious expression of anger at authority that arises partly from the excitement of the game but is largely a residue from daily living. So why should I let their booing affect my performance? More importantly, why should I allow their booing to affect how I feel about myself?

—*Impartial Judgment*, with Glenn Dickey

Leader Uniforms?

You are more likely to be objective and less likely to blow your stack if you can recognize the difference between your *self* and your *role*. Folks don't yell at me on the football field because I'm Travis Collins; they yell because I have on stripes. In fact, when I put on those knickers and my cleats and my striped shirt, I physically take on a different persona. At my core I am obviously the same person, but in my capacity as an official my role is specialized. I've put on a different hat. Literally. When I take on that persona, it's much easier to let the criticism roll off my shoulder like water off a duck's back. I know they are yelling at "the official," and I just happen to be in that role.

Maybe leadership would be less stressful if we had leader uniforms. What if we all had to wear, say, plaid jackets, when we are in leadership roles? Then we might be more able to distinguish between our function as leaders and our identity as persons. Every time we put on that plaid jacket we'd know that we were assuming a particular role, and we might just remember the distinction between that *role* and who we *are*.

As mentioned above, some people simply have a deep resentment toward authority figures, so it comes naturally for them to dislike the spiritual leader. I had breakfast the other day with Dr. Bruce Heilman, current chancellor and former president of the University of Richmond. As we talked about leadership, he told me his life changed significantly for the better when he realized that those folks giving him such a hard time really were not attacking *him*; they were attacking *the office of the president*. That realization allowed him to receive unhappy visitors and hear them out without internalizing all their burdens and grievances. He didn't take their attacks personally.

It's Not About You

It's also far easier to be objective about criticism if you recognize that the real issue might have nothing to do with you. Maybe the one who is so critical toward you has personal problems.

I was walking down the hall of a nursing home one day when I noticed up ahead a middle-aged woman pushing an elderly woman in a wheelchair. Even before I reached them the elderly lady, obviously a resident at the nursing home, called out to me.

"Aren't you going to speak to me? You'd better not ignore me!" (She apparently thought I was an acquaintance who was snubbing her, though I had never seen her before.)

So I walked over and apologized so to speak. I asked her how she was doing, and we made small talk (although I could tell she was still unhappy with me). I was wearing a Polo shirt with a horse on the chest. She asked, "What's that on your shirt, an ink spot?"

"No ma'am," I said, "that's a horse."

Trying to be cute, I added, "This is my *cowboy* shirt!"

A scowl fell over the elderly lady's face. "Well, that's a good shirt for you," she said, "you old mule!"

Only she didn't say *mule*.

She attacked my dignity! But did I get angry at her? No, of course not. I could see that she had problems completely unrelated to me. What she said wasn't about me at all.

It might be that when someone attacks you, it's not about you at all. It might be that he or she is emotionally hurting or unhealthy, perhaps insecure or unhappy, and fighting to establish a sense of worth. Maybe there are problems at home, or at work, and you might just be a convenient tin can to kick!

James 4:1 reminds us that battles between us are usually the result of battles within us. "What causes fights and quarrels among you? Don't they come from your desires that battle within you?" The person with whom you are having a conflict might be experiencing inner turmoil. So, if people hurt you, let your reaction be tempered by the awareness that you might not be the problem at all.

Just for Vocational Ministers

I can think of no other leaders whose identity is so closely tied to their professional titles as vocational ministers. Far more than most people, we tend to think we *are* what we *do*. Unfortunately, that means it's easy for us to take opposition personally.

One answer to that is to find a life outside of our professional roles. That's one reason why football officiating is so good for me, and that's also a reason I enjoy writing. I'd encourage you, too, to find some hobby or avocation that you really enjoy. People who do not have a life outside their ministries tend to forget the difference between who they are and what they do. Such folks are in danger of committing several sins, including: becoming arrogant when things are going well, believing that they should be credited for the success; and becoming depressed when things are not going as well as expected, because their ego strength comes solely from their work/ministry.

So find some hobbies. Learn to find fulfillment in a variety of things. Don't lose yourself in any activity or organization, including ministry. Find something that is completely unrelated to your ministerial identity. That might keep criticism from getting under your skin.

14

Unmet Expectations

In *The Umpire Strikes Back*, coauthored with David Fisher, the late Major League umpire Ron Luciano quipped:

> *Umpiring is best described as the profession of standing between two seven year olds with one ice cream cone. No matter how good an umpire you are, your entire career is going to be spent making fifty percent of all the players and managers unhappy.*

While our leadership satisfaction rating should be higher than that of baseball umpires, it's still true that we can't make everyone happy all the time. That's a hard lesson for some of us to learn.

Twenty years ago I took a personality inventory, and it showed that I was very sensitive to how I am perceived by others. I took the same instrument a few years ago and found out that, among other things, I am now more likely to make a decision based on what I believe is right rather than on how

I think it will affect people's opinion of me.

Experts say that our personalities do not vary much throughout our lives. I believe any change in my personality has come from the pressures of leadership. I think I just decided at a subconscious level that if I were going to lead with an undue concern for people's perceptions of me I would either fold under the pressure or lose my sanity.

Maybe my personality, my preference, hasn't really changed at all. Maybe I'm just choosing (again, at a subconscious level) to operate as one who is more interested in my convictions than in what others might think. Whichever is the case, I've had to get comfortable with the fact that I cannot live out my values and, at the same time, meet everyone's expectations.

Truth is, I'd prefer to do what I feel is right *and* have everybody think I'm wonderful all the time. It's just that I never have had that choice.

Not Living Up to Expectations

Our family moved from Kentucky to Virginia during the summer before our oldest son's senior year in high school. Normally that would be a terrible time to make a move, but our kids have an MK (missionary-kid) mentality, and Landon actually thought the move would be an adventure. And it did go well; he even won the job of starting quarterback on the football team, providing him instant friends and a ready-made role.

Word of Landon's coming preceded us. The football program was abuzz about the impending arrival of a star athlete from Kentucky. But the info that got out was not completely accurate.

Expectations were high before Landon arrived. I remember conversations in which fathers said to me, "Oh, we've heard about Landon! We hear he's the real deal!" I thought, *Well, he's the real deal to me, but your expectations might be too high.*

People heard that Landon was an all-district player in Kentucky. And that was true. He was all-district—but as a place kicker, not a quarterback. Word got out that he was in the Kentucky high school record books. And that was true—but his name was there for kicking 11 extra points in one game, not for passing or running the football.

Quite candidly, as the season progressed, people were disappointed in Landon's performance as a quarterback. He did well, but he didn't live up to the over-hyped and unrealistic expectations. That was tough on Landon. I remember one night when Landon was really discouraged. He wept as he said, "People expected too much." Still, Landon kept his head up and did the best he could, making me far prouder than if he'd been an all-state player with a bad attitude.

Landon learned an important lesson during that season: Living up to people's expectations is impossible. And if you obsess over living up to those expectations—if you live for the acceptance, approval, and admiration of other people—you will make yourself miserable.

And not only that, you also will be tempted to do things you don't want to do to impress people you don't even like. If you aren't careful you will do the wrong things for the wrong reasons for the wrong people.

Teresa McBean serves on the ministry staff at the church where I pastor. During her high school days, she was in the school choir. Every day during one school year, as she walked down the hall toward the choir room, she would pass by a gathering of several football players. And every day for a long time a girl from the special education class would be dancing for the football players, who often would throw change at her. One day Teresa overheard one of the football players telling the mentally challenged young lady, "If you dance we'll be your friends!"

Teresa pulled the young lady aside and said to her, "You don't have to dance for those guys. And they are not your friends."

This girl didn't want to dance. But she was willing to do it because she thought she was earning the friendship and admiration—the applause—of those jocks.

You, too, are going to be tempted to dance for people in order to earn their admiration. Identify that temptation, understand it, and refuse to acquiesce to it. Be all you were created to be. Do what you know deep in your heart to be right. And don't obsess over others' expectations of your leadership. Beware not to violate your values in order to hear a little applause. The call to spiritual leadership is a call to shun the unhealthy longing for approval.

Aiming to Please Whom?

But, of course, neither are we called to callously disregard the opinions of others. So, what is the answer?

I believe the answer is in the words of the missionary and spiritual leader, Paul, "We speak as men approved by God to be entrusted with the gospel. We are not trying to please men but God, who tests our hearts" (1 Thessalonians 2:3–4). There were folks who claimed that Paul had no right to preach to them or teach them. After all, he had persecuted Christians, even to death. His critics may have charged: "You used to hunt Christians down! What right do you have to lead us?"

Furthermore, his message, like that of Jesus, was of grace—God's unconditional, undeserved, unlimited love. Many religious leaders of the day taught a legalistic approach to religion: *If you keep all the rules God will accept you.* So when Paul preached freedom and faith and grace, legalists opposed him by every means available to them.

Besides that, there were people who didn't like Paul's leadership style. Some said he was just trying to trick them with flattery. Others, almost certainly, may have thought he was too aggressive and inflexible.

So what was Paul's response? His response was, "I cannot please everyone...so I'll just do my best to please God."

There often are persons, or groups of persons, whom we allow to have great influence on us. We value their opinions highly, and what they think about us makes a great difference to us. Their opinion of us is so important that our sense of worth comes largely from their approval or disapproval, from their applause or their jeers. But playing to any human audience will never bring ultimate satisfaction. We cannot, and were never intended to, meet all their expectations of us. Thus Paul's approach: "I'm not trying to please people, but God."

Forgive the truism, but you simply cannot live to meet others' expectations. Jesus himself couldn't, and didn't try. Of Jesus we read:

The people were looking for him and when they came to where he was, they tried to keep him from leaving them.

But he said, "I must preach the good news of the kingdom of God to the other towns also, because that is why I was sent."
—Luke 4:42–43

Know your calling. Know why you were sent. And then don't allow yourself to be sidetracked by others' demands of you.

Just for Vocational Ministers

Studies have shown that vocational ministers tend to have personalities that loathe conflict. We like to please people. Conflict, therefore, is harder for most of us than for other leaders. But leading a church or other Christian organization requires a mature perspective on conflict and an intentional willingness to face it. The sooner you understand that you cannot please everyone, the sooner you will be able to make courageous decisions and sleep well at night.

15

Dealing with Criticism

L eadership depends on an individual's ability to function effectively in spite of controversy. Most of us never will (in fact, never *should*) completely get over the pain of complaints and criticisms. If we don't at least wince from the sting of critical barbs, then maybe our hearts have become too hard.

Nevertheless, our goal cannot be to avoid criticism. Ray Pritchard and the late Bob Briner observed that the ability, or lack of ability, to face criticism well is a key factor in determining whether or not a person is cut out to lead:

> Some are not temperamentally suited to handle opposition, which comes even in the face of pure motives and quality, effective action; these people are not suited to be leaders because they are unwilling to pay the emotional price required when attacked while doing good. This is OK. Not all are called to be leaders. In fact, this is a good test of leadership: can you handle unwarranted criticism?
> —The Leadership Lessons of Jesus

Criticism Is Inevitable

People sometimes ask if it bothers me when fans yell at me while I'm officiating. The truth is that it almost never gets to me. I guess there are two reasons for that. First, I don't know them and they don't know me, so it's not personal. Second, I expect it; hot heads are as much a part of the game as hot dogs and hot chocolate. Of course there are boundaries, but criticism is part of the experience. In any profession, if you do just about anything of note you will receive some sort of censure, either mild or harsh, particularly if you hold some type of supervisory, managerial, or leadership role. Your effectiveness as a leader will depend largely on how you respond to that criticism.

While there is no virtue in relishing opposition, a longing to be admired can cost you your integrity. Jesus himself warned: "Woe to you when all men speak well of you" (Luke 6:26). Criticism, therefore, should be accepted as a cost of leadership. Here are some thoughts on handling criticism:

• **Criticism is not all bad.** Criticism can be a good thing. It can be like those kiddy bumpers in the lanes at the bowling alley. Criticism, at least accurate criticism, keeps us headed toward the goal. It certainly is easier to be humble when we are being criticized, and proper humility is a good thing. Criticism also initiates the kind of intense self-examination that leadership always requires. Moreover, criticism forces us to ask what God thinks of us. Therefore, criticism is not all bad.

Criticism makes us alert to our vulnerabilities, and thus can be valuable. For example, in our previous house the thermostat was on the wall directly across from our fireplace. When the fire was on, the thermostat received that warm input and shut off the heating unit. It was comfortable in front of the fire, but if you walked into another area of the house you'd notice a big drop in the temperature. That thermostat was receiving warm input from the fire but did not register how chilly it was in the back bedrooms.

Thus it is with the leader who receives only warm, fuzzy input. He or she is unaware of the cold rooms in the organization—those issues and relationships that need attention. If someone sounds a critical alarm, that signals there may be problems in areas or rooms we don't normally frequent. So, criticism is, or at least can be, a good thing.

● **Be thick-skinned, but not calloused.** Over the years I have begun to lead more with my head than my heart, so I have developed a good deal of resistance to the pain of criticism. I didn't make the shift consciously; I think that evolution in personality came from being criticized and then realizing that I'd never survive with thin skin. And I have been blessed with the leadership of healthy congregations! Thin skin is going to be particularly problematic for those of you who lead dysfunctional groups.

Just make sure your thick skin doesn't grow calloules. In *Leadership on the Line*, Ronald A. Heifetz and Marty Linsky warn:

> *It is too easy to buy in to the common myth that you cannot survive a demanding professional role without a tough exterior, as if you have to check your compassion at the office door. Calloused fingertips lose their sensitivity. Your listening becomes less and less acute, until you fail to hear the real messages from people around you, and cannot identify the songs beneath their words . . . In the*

effort to protect yourself, you risk numbing yourself to the world in which you are embedded.

The authors go on to write that one of the keys to leadership is dealing with stress and distress without yielding to the temptation to become numb and hardened. The antidote, they say, is a sacred heart: "A sacred heart means you may feel tortured and betrayed, powerless and hopeless, and yet stay open. It's the capacity to encompass the entire range of your human experience without hardening or closing yourself."

• **Look behind and beneath the criticism.** When someone jumps you, berates you, or criticizes you, just remember (or try to find out) where they are coming from. And that might make the harsh words easier to accept.

There are people who will make life hard for you today, and they will be making life hard for someone else tomorrow. Some folks have a track record of bad relationships. It also might be that the people making life hard for you are living under a heavy load themselves, one that has nothing to do with you. They might be unhappy because of personal issues. There might be problems at home, or with someone else at work, and you just happen to be on the receiving end of their venting.

The February 24, 1997, issue of *Newsweek* carried a memorable, tragic-but-true story. Max Dadashvili was sitting at a table in a sidewalk café in Tel Aviv. High above him, a 72-year-old man decided life was no longer worth living and threw himself off the building. The suicidal septuagenarian landed on Dadashvili. One moment he is sipping on his coffee; the next moment he is on the ground with a suicide jumper on top of him. Dadashvili's back was broken; the

TOUGH CALLS

jumper walked away uninjured. The 26-year-old Dadashvili later lamented, "I can't understand my rotten luck."

Sometimes you get hurt by other people's attempts to deal with their own pain. The firestorm you find yourself in is an awkward attempt by a hurting person to do something about his or her inner turmoil. You just happen to be in the wrong place at the wrong time. It's like the guy who gets yelled at by his boss, then yells at his secretary who yells at the guy at the mailroom who yells at the parking attendant who goes home and kicks the dog. The poor dog had nothing to do with it!

Of course there are some people who are just plain mean. There are those who seem to take delight in hurting other people. They are happiest when people around them are unhappy. The psalmist describes his nemeses in Psalm 59: "Fierce men conspire against me...They return at evening, snarling like dogs, and prowl about the city" (59:3,6). Some folks have the temperament of an animal on the prowl. They seem to have a snarl on their face; they look vicious. And they always seem to be on the lookout for new prey.

If someone attacks you, let your reaction be tempered by an understanding of your antagonist's personality and context. Have the maturity to discern whether this is a reasonable person or a habitual malcontent.

A leader must also try to determine the motive of the critic. If the one criticizing you has your good at heart, then that person's criticism deserves a more careful hearing than the criticism of one who wishes to wound you. You simply must do your best to discern the motives of the critical party.

It won't take away the sting of harsh words. But it might

lessen the sting… if you will try to look beneath the surface.

- **Be willing to listen.** If we are not careful, we could eventually start to dismiss negative opinions as irrelevant and uninformed. That would be unfortunate, for sometimes the criticism is valid. We, as leaders, need to be able to listen, for our sake and for the sake of the one criticizing.

Of course criticism is not always constructive. Some criticism is completely unfounded, is inappropriate, and should be treated as such. Yet much criticism has some helpful element to it, and hearing it can be good. We can't automatically dismiss people who complain or confront us. That would be arrogant.

By the way, an important benefit of listening to criticism is that the act of listening often disarms the assailant. When you hear him or her out, you can almost see that person loosening the gunbelt and laying the guns on the table. When leaders listen, they can usually defuse a potentially explosive situation; and then something constructive actually can happen.

What other people think does matter. Leaders cannot afford to be aloof or dismissive.

- **Respond only when appropriate.** Sports officials can't stop the game to answer every criticism. There are times, however, when an explanation to a head coach is warranted. One of the skills a leader must develop is the discernment to know when to ignore criticism and when to answer it. I've found the following rules of thumb helpful.

  1. If there is a pretty good chance you have made a mistake, a time-out to correct it is in order.
  2. If the health of the organization is threatened by the criticism of your leadership, some sort of

response is necessary. As an official, I certainly don't react to the jeers from the stands, and I even will overlook a lot of complaints from the coach. However, when the "c" word—*cheating*—is used or even implied, the one who used it is almost always going to get an unsportsmanlike penalty. When anyone implies that the officials are crooked, the integrity of the game itself is threatened. Likewise, when someone's attacks exceed the limits of legitimate criticism, threatening the very health of the organization, some sort of measured response is likely necessary.

3. In a football game, the head coach is the one who can get my attention. I can't pay attention to the fans, the trainers, the water boys ("hydration managers," as some like to be called), the substitutes on the sidelines, or even the assistant coaches. Only the head coach can call a time-out to challenge the decision of an official. Most folks I ignore; I pay attention to the head coach.

Leaders need to know or decide who warrants their attention. I'm not talking about just the movers and shakers. I'm talking about those voices that need to be heard—the influencers, the wise, the experienced, the ones who have your best interests and those of the organization at heart.

Just for Vocational Ministers

Criticism seems particularly agonizing for minister-types. We want folks to think well of us, and disapproval causes us to break out in hives.

Could some of our distaste for criticism also be rooted in a belief that our divine call somehow places us above accountability? In an email he sent me recently, my friend and fellow pastor, George Mason, articulates well the truth that someone called by God answers ultimately to God Himself. Yet he balances that truth with the fact that there is both a contractual and covenantal agreement between the vocational minister and the organization to which he or she is related:

> One reason we are ordained to the gospel ministry and receive self-employment status is to make clear that our primary calling is to serve God always and wherever we are, regardless of what paid relationships we may have with a church or institution. Thus, we are never employees, strictly speaking. We are always serving the Lord in either a contractual way or covenantal way with some entity, but this does not affect our call, only the location of it . . . On occasion I have reminded myself, and on occasion I have reminded deacons and personnel committees that I do not work for them; I work for God with and alongside them, and that only as long as together we deem it fitting.

The contractual and covenantal relationship that Mason mentions gives the organization the right and responsibility to hold ministers accountable. Spiritual leaders do have authority granted by God and affirmed by God's people. But that authority does not place us above or beyond legitimate questions and criticisms.

I have found that some vocational ministers resent accountability and the criticism that often accompanies it. Some have the idea that they answer only and directly to God, and that no other human has a right to evaluate them. I remember one pastor whom I heard preach more than once about the danger of "touching God's anointed." He loved to preach from Psalm 105:15, "Do not touch my anointed ones; do my prophets no harm." One time he preached on the prophet Elisha and the boys who harassed Elisha, found in 2 Kings 2. Remember the story? After Elisha turned and called down a curse in the name of the Lord, two bears came out of the woods and mauled those 42 ill-mannered adolescents. Now that will get a kid's attention!

Although I was young at the time, I sensed that this preacher had a real accountability problem. I didn't know all that was going on in the church, but these recurring sermons about the authority of the pastor and the danger of opposing him made me wonder what it was from which he was trying to shield himself.

Accountability includes the possibility of criticism and even discipline. If I don't fulfill my responsibilities as pastor, the appropriate leaders of our church have the right to initiate some sort of corrective measures. That might mean putting me on probation. I certainly don't automatically merit a raise each year, even if the finances are strong. It might even mean I will be relieved of my duties.

If I'm going to lead, I'm going to be held accountable. And if I'm going to be held accountable, I'm going to be criticized. Yes, even in the church.

16

Worth
Fighting For

Some folks just aren't cut out to be sports officials. There are a lot of very good people, who are talented in many areas, who would become faint at the kind of abuse that officials often take from parents, fans, and coaches. A person who cannot withstand that level of conflict should not even put on the striped shirt.

And the truth is that a lot of very good people are not called or equipped to be in leadership positions. One of the tests of the calling to leadership is this: can the person bear up under the disappointment and disapproval that often accompany leadership? Is rejection a significant fear? Is loneliness unduly painful? If so, then there are many places to contribute besides at the helm of the ship, especially if the ship is headed toward rough waters. If criticism and conflict are overly distressing to you, then your leadership opportunities will be limited to situations that have a "low heat setting," as my friend Ann Perkins calls them.

Don't Look for Conflict

God tells us, in Romans 12:18, "If it is possible, as far as it depends on you, live at peace with everyone." As we will see in a moment, living at peace with everyone is not possible for leaders. Nevertheless, leaders who actually prefer conflict to harmony fall short of God's plan and jeopardize their organizations.

Abraham Lincoln recommended that people let little differences blow over—not to make major controversies out of minor disagreements. He said, "A man has not time to spend half his life in quarrels...No man resolved to make the most of himself, can spare time for personal contention" (from Donald T. Phillips' *Lincoln on Leadership*). Conflict uses up a lot of our time and energy. It's emotionally and even physically unhealthy. So let's not go around looking for trouble.

Nevertheless, trouble will come, and the truth is that conflict is not always all bad.

Conflict Will Look for You

If you are called to lead, you can expect that things will heat up, so let's expand our discussion beyond just criticism to include interpersonal conflict.

• **Conflict is inevitable, and it's not the worst thing that could happen.** I find Proverbs 14:4 compelling: "Where no oxen are, the manger is clean, But much revenue *comes* by the strength of the ox" (NASB).

The first church I served as pastor was near Upton, Kentucky. One of the families in that community was surnamed Rider. The Riders had a dairy farm with award-winning Jersey cows. The Riders went to the Kentucky State Fair every year and always brought home enough trophies and ribbons to fill a hay wagon. They won awards for having the prettiest cows, the most-milk-giving cows, and the cows with the best calves.

They never did, however, get a prize for clean stalls.

I noticed that whenever I stopped by the Rider farm, the men who worked in the barn always had on high rubber boots. They were not wearing that footwear as a fashion statement. They wore those boots because prize-winning cows make for messy stalls.

The Riders' farm produced truckloads of milk and beautiful cattle. But if the Riders had decided to make pristine barns a priority, their farm would not have been very productive. Good, milk-producing cows require cleaning out messy stalls.

And any organization that is going to be effective in the twenty-first century will have to understand the inevitability of some messiness. A rapidly changing world means that organizational leadership, in every field I can think of, is getting more and more complicated. Thus it is truer than ever, that if the leader does almost anything of note, there will be conflict.

- **Conflict is preferable to plateau and decline.** I was about six weeks into my second pastorate when an issue arose that I knew could be divisive. I didn't know whether to take a stand or just let things play out. So I called a certain pastor and asked for some advice. He gave me some good words: "There are very few issues worth dividing a church."

I took his advice. I held onto those words. I quoted him a number of times.

That pastor lived by that philosophy. He has since retired and, in fact, the church he led never divided. They were relatively controversy-free during his long tenure. The pastor had a calm demeanor and was inoffensive. He avoided controversy and was never involved in any kind of major fracas. I have followed that pastor's former congregation over the years, and there has still never been a major uproar.

The church, however, has never gotten off its plateau. The pastor did a great job of shepherding and comforting, yet I believe more assertive leadership could have better served the church in the long run.

There are indeed very few things worth splitting a church over, and broken relationships in any organization are regrettable. But a peace-first mind-set, taken to the extreme, will result in no aggressive plans, no changes, no risks. A commitment to keeping the peace at all costs can rob people and organizations of their mission. When any organization becomes so obsessed with avoiding division that they do nothing, they have missed the point. Many organizations that pride themselves on peace and harmony are dying on the vine. There's no risk, and no growth.

It would have been far more tranquil at the temple that day had Jesus chosen not to turn over those tables and drive out the money changers. Tranquility, however, is not the ultimate goal.

- **Conflict can be good for an organization.** An old saying reminds us, "When two partners agree, one of them is unnecessary." Disputes help everyone to look at the issue in a new way. Disagreements force organizations to think through a controversial issue. Conflict might just be a sign that, for key people in the organization, the mission is more important than superficial harmony.

Peace at Any Cost?

Progress often brings some division; tough calls divide people. Even Jesus declared, "I did not come to bring peace, but a sword" (Matthew 10:34). Jesus knew that radical obedience to Him would result in conflict.

I like it when people like me, and I like it even better when people are getting along. I am increasingly aware, however, that neither my personal popularity nor congregational concord should be my highest priority.

The popular book by Tom Brokaw, *The Greatest Generation*, has a chapter about Andy Rooney, the well-known television commentator. During World War II, Rooney served in the Army as a war reporter with *Stars and Stripes*, the Army's newspaper. He was present in 1944 on the day that Paris was liberated by the Allies. He also crossed over into Germany and reached Buchenwald, one of the Nazi concentration camps. There he witnessed what he had only heard rumored. He saw firsthand the evils that had been occurring there, and he said, "I was ashamed of myself for ever having considered refusing to serve in the Army. For the first time I knew that any peace is not better than any war." Rooney was right. Peace at any cost is not worth the cost.

Just for Vocational Ministers

When I was interviewing with the pastoral search team from my current church, Bon Air Baptist, we talked about my personality type. They knew me to be the type of person who dislikes conflict, so they asked if that aspect of my personality would hamper my leadership. I acknowledged that the dread of disapproval could be my Achilles heel. Yet together we recognized that leadership requires courage—including the courage to do what one believes is right even when opposition is both painful and inevitable. I honestly told them, "I don't like conflict, but I choose not to be derailed by it. Conflict and criticism are prices I will pay in an effort to be an effective leader."

SECTION FIVE
PEOPLE ISSUES

But avoid foolish controversies and genealogies and arguments and quarrels about the law, because these are unprofitable and useless. Warn a divisive person once, and then warn him a second time. After that, have nothing to do with him. You may be sure that such a man is warped and sinful; he is self-condemned.
—Titus 3:9–11

17

You Gotta Call Unsportsmanlike Conduct

Some fouls can be overlooked. Maybe a simple holding foul occurs 30 yards behind the run. I'm probably not going to throw a flag on the one who committed the foul; I'll warn him, but a flag would be unnecessary. Maybe the third-string wide receiver is not lined up correctly, and his team is losing 50 to 0 with 30 seconds to play. I'm probably not going to blow the whistle and stop the clock because that player is technically out of position. If I were to do that my fellow officials would give me the evil eye.

Not *every* foul deserves a penalty. Unsportsmanlike conduct, however, must be called, or else the officials will lose control of the game. Football is an intense, aggressive sport, and a fracas is often just one provocative comment away. So officials have to be on top of confrontational situations.

Unsportsmanlike conduct is intolerable in any organization. Even in tense, pressurized situations, the leader must insist on respect between individuals. The only time I ever remember chastising someone in public was when that person spoke inappropriately to a member of our support staff.

Civility Is Not Negotiable

Trash talk on the field can seem harmless at first. But unsportsmanlike conduct can get ugly in a hurry, so it can't be allowed. The official must act decisively to prevent the escalation of conflict; if he ignores taunts and offensive gestures and other abuses, then that official becomes responsible for the game's deterioration.

In *The Official's Role in Improving Sportsmanship*, Barry Mano, president of the National Association of Sports Officials, laments the fact that officials seem to be going soft on sportsmanship. He calls it a trend toward "the kinder, gentler official," and contends that it is a dangerously downward trend. Many officials seem not to want to call unsportsmanlike conduct penalties because they don't want to be thought of as the bad guys. But if officials tolerate antagonism, Mano insists, they "could rapidly turn sports into a wasteland of poor behavior." The application to spiritual leadership is obvious: if we do not address and curtail disrespectful behavior, we are jeopardizing the health and mission of the organizations we lead.

The stakes are too high for any organization to be dominated by people who ignore or violate the organization's vision and values. Sometimes we must confront. Whenever we confront we must do it carefully, with mature, Christ-like attitudes. But mature leaders have to make it crystal clear that the mission is too important to allow it to be jeopardized by divisive persons. And sometimes being frank is the only effective approach. Even Jesus Himself said, "Woe to you, teachers of the law and Pharisees, you hypocrites! You are like whitewashed tombs" (Matthew 23:27). Jesus knew when not to pull punches.

So, for the sake of the organization you lead, you have to throw a flag when people act in a mean-spirited way. You cannot allow the bad behavior of a bully, or the monkey business of malcontents, to contaminate the whole. When you see disruptive behavior, you've got to call it for what it is. You cannot let your fear of the fallout, or your terror of the tyrant, prevent you from intervening when someone is causing trouble.

One of the most important responsibilities of a leader is maintaining the organization's "cultural harmony," as Max De Pree puts it. You must protect those you lead from the disruptive acts of hurtful people. That responsibility cannot be abdicated and cannot be delegated. The health of your organization and the emotional well-being of employees hang in the balance. You've simply got to call unsportsmanlike conduct.

Healthy Tension or Disruptive Conflict?

Before moving on I want to point out that it is *malice*, not appropriate debate and disagreement, that leaders must try to curtail. Some confrontations among those we lead are healthy and do not violate the principles of moral conduct. Right and proper confrontation shouldn't be discouraged.

Dick Burleson was an SEC football referee for 25 years. In his book, *"You Better Be Right!"*, he relates one of his favorite stories, an incident from the 1987 Alabama-Penn State game.

Alabama's All-American linebacker, Derrick Thomas, had just leveled Penn State's quarterback. The hit was clean, purely according to the rules, and not at all illegal. It was ferocious, nonetheless.

As the Penn State team huddled up, Burleson noticed that the players were looking over to their sideline and raising their arms to signal they didn't know what was going on. Finally they asked Burleson for a time-out, and said, "We can't find our quarterback!" Joe Paterno and company were looking everywhere along the Penn State sideline but couldn't locate the missing player! Finally Burleson spotted the absentee QB wandering among the Alabama defensive backs. The referee ran to the young man and noticed a faraway look in his eyes.

"Son, are you all right?" Burleson asked. "Yes, sir," answered the rattled Penn State signal-caller, "I'm just trying to find the huddle."

Here's my point: Burleson didn't penalize Derrick Thomas for the tackle although the blow must have caused a gasp from some of the onlookers. It was legal, appropriate, within the guidelines of the game. Likewise, sometimes the people you lead will confront their peers in completely appropriate ways. The "tackle" will be "clean," but because many people equate conflict with impropriety, someone in the organization you lead is likely to become faint at the sight of open disagreement. One of the spiritual leader's responsibilities is to help people see that confrontation can be helpful. In fact, an unwillingness to address tough topics makes for superficial relationships, or worse. At times you will have to insist that certain issues be discussed, because, if unaddressed, they will simmer and cause serious underlying tension.

One of your most important and challenging duties as a spiritual leader is to discern between healthy tension and destructive conflict. If you are going to negotiate conflict, you will have to allow for disagreement. Yet you cannot allow attacks to get personal, calculating, or tasteless. Distinguishing between healthy and unhealthy conflict (often with no more to go on than intuition) will be one of your most critical responsibilities.

You've got to call unsportsmanlike conduct, but when *appropriate* confrontations occur, help those you lead see the value of saying tough things in the right way.

Just for Vocational Ministers

Bon Air Baptist's pastor emeritus, Bob Cochran, told me a sobering story that drives home why we need to nip incendiary practices in the bud. Many years ago, a young man stood on the grounds of the church where Bob was then pastor, put a gun to his head, and took his life. By the time Bob arrived on the scene the young man's body had been removed, but when the pastor went to the spot where the awful event had taken place he spotted an autumn leaf covered with that young man's blood. Bob immediately recalled Genesis 4:10, "Your brother's blood cries out to Me from the ground."

This young man, you see, had visited the church. They had his name in their prospect file. But they were too distracted to reach out to him. They were in the middle of one of those all-too-common afflictions of local congregations—a church fight. They were too preoccupied with the dissension to make the young man a priority.

Bob kept the leaf, had it pressed and framed under glass, and hung it on the wall opposite his desk. I have held that bloodstained, prophetic leaf. Decades later it still bears traces of that young man's blood and declares: We can't in-fight and out-reach at the same time.

The stakes in our churches and other Christian organization are too great for us to allow someone's ruthless behavior to divide and distract us from our mission. I do not want to stand before God on Judgment Day and have Him say, "I gave you the opportunity to lead a great Christian organization, and you blew it by not protecting its fellowship."

18

Handling Troublemakers

Coaches aren't any more quarrelsome than any other segment of the population. In fact, one could argue that their interest in young people is a sure sign that most coaches are men and women of outstanding character. We all admire the volunteer hours spent by recreational league coaches. And everyone knows that what high school coaches get paid probably doesn't even cover their expenses. Furthermore, fans often criticize coaches even more harshly than officials. Fans often second-guess the coaches with a confidence that is laughable. Coaches deserve a lot of credit for their willingness to put up with that.

The vast majority of the coaches pacing the sidelines are outstanding folks. It is an honor for players to play for them, and for officials to officiate for them.

But of course every profession or avocation has its difficult personalities, and coaching is no exception. (Neither is officiating, I might add.) And the high intensity of athletic contests, together with such things as fierce rivalries, close scores, and the pressure to win, combine to form the perfect storms of conflict between officials and coaches. Sometimes coaches cross the line.

On a few occasions I've had to say, "Coach, that's enough. No more." I have let him have his say. He's registered his complaint. But he has crossed the line, and my next move will be to "flag" him. He has become a troublemaker and is now jeopardizing the game. It is my responsibility to put a stop to it.

Three Bad Choices

Differing backgrounds, personality types, needs, and tastes, coupled with people's passion for the company or institution, make conflict unavoidable. Leaders have a choice, however, in how they will handle the conflict. There are a number of popular, but poor, means of handling conflict, including: (1) avoiding the issue, hoping it will go away; (2) courting controversy; and (3) compromise.

First, avoidance is not an effective strategy. Waiting for the right time to intervene *is* a good strategy, but crossing your fingers and burying your head in the sand is *not*. Troublemakers generally don't go away on their own.

Second, courting controversy is just plain foolish. A few folks have martyr complexes and feel somehow validated when they are in conflict with someone. If you find yourself looking for a good fight, you need to rethink your leadership style.

The third approach—compromise—seems the least of these evils. Yet compromise—at least the kind of compromise that risks the organization's values—can be devastating to an organization. There are values that just shouldn't be open to negotiation.

Furthermore, olive branches often don't work on die-hard troublemakers. Disrupters probably will not respond to kindness, at least in the short run, no matter how noble your intentions. So, if none of these three choices is the right approach, then what is a leader to do?

Going by the Book

Paul wrote to Titus, "Warn a divisive person once, and then warn him a second time. After that, have nothing to do with him" (Titus 3:10). Sometimes leadership requires painful confrontation. Whenever we confront, we must do it carefully, with mature, Christ-like attitudes, and only after honest self-examination. Even so, mature leaders sometimes have to say, "That's enough. No more."

There are times when we have to let people be people. All of us are going to lose our patience and say something out of line now and then. But when someone is being destructive—when the organization is suffering because of someone's belligerence, then it is time to say, "We cannot let you get away with that."

Remember, I'm not talking here about someone who merely disagrees with the leader's opinion. I'm talking about a real live troublemaker—any person who has, over time, developed a pattern of division, a reputation for antagonism, a habit of stirring things up and injuring the community or organization.

If a person has caused enough trouble enough times, then it becomes the responsibility of the organization's leadership to intervene following the guidelines of Titus 3:10, beginning with warnings. These warnings should be private, involving only a handful of leaders (people recognized as standard bearers for the organization, for example). Then, if the trouble continues, there should follow some sort of censure. Such disciplinary action must be redemptive, not destructive, in nature, and it must be rooted in compassion.

However, that compassion must never allow the proverbial tail to wag the dog. Negative people—whiners and controllers—must not be allowed to set the agenda for the organization. It is even more important that the leader intervene when bullying is the issue. If we let people get away with mistreating others, we allow the victims of their abuse to feel devalued.

There Must Be Consequences

There was an interesting article in *Referee* magazine in August 2004 titled, "For the Fourth Time, That's Enough!" Tim Sloan writes that neither repeated warnings, dirty looks, soft voices, nor loud voices are effective in handling a coach or player who is out of line, unless there are consequences to his behavior.

"Warnings," writes Sloan, "are not enforcement. Technical fouls, red cards, and ejections are."

Sloan makes an important point for leaders: if we are going to deal effectively with troublemakers, we are going to have to levy some kind of consequences.

Dysfunctional tyrants must be stopped, even if it means they quit the company, leave the church, or get fired. Jesus told us to be "gentle as doves," but in that same sentence he cautioned us to be "wise as serpents" (Matthew 10:16).

In Calvin Miller's *The Empowered Leader*, Norm Evans (a Christian gentleman and former offensive lineman with the

Miami Dolphins) tells about a football player who went to his coach and complained about a player on the opposing team.

"He keeps pulling my helmet over my eyes. What should I do?"

The wise coach answered simply, "Don't let him do it!"

It is Christian to turn the other cheek. But it is not good spiritual leadership to let someone wreak havoc on the group. I believe if we were to pray and say, "God, that guy keeps causing trouble. What should I do?" God would answer, "Don't let him do it!"

Of course it's easy for me to sit here with my hands on a keyboard telling you to stand up to that belligerent troublemaker in your organization. Truth is, I know it's not pleasant to take on intimidating people. Nevertheless, if you are in a leadership role then you have to deal firmly with difficult personalities.

Throw the Flag Early

As an official, I often work as the head linesman, which puts me near the sideline looking down the line of scrimmage. That also means I am the official (along with my counterpart across the field, the line judge) closest to the coaches and the bench.

On occasion, the coaches and/or players get out of hand. It might be as innocuous as them inching their way onto the field in all the excitement; or it might be as serious as them making slanderous remarks about the officials. One of my responsibilities is to keep those on my sideline under control, and the yellow flag is my only real tool in doing that.

In the pregame—the officials' conference before the

contest—we review rules and discuss mechanics (how we position ourselves based on particular plays). We also anticipate potential scenarios and discuss how we should handle them. In regard to controlling the sidelines, I've heard referees say dozens of times, "If you're going to hit 'em, hit 'em early." In other words, don't overlook inappropriate comments and behavior from the coaches and players for half the game and then throw a flag; throw it before it gets out of hand.

I have been guilty at times, I'll admit, of waiting too late to "hit 'em" on the sidelines. I've pretended I didn't hear scathing insults for three quarters and then decided I've had my fill in the fourth. But by that time the situation is my fault, and I'm not going to throw a flag that late in the game for something I should have addressed long before it got out of hand. I've had to put up with some rough talk in the fourth quarter of some games because I didn't flag the offenders earlier.

Likewise, ignoring problems in our organizations, hoping they will magically go away, is a reflection of poor leadership. Leaders have to nip trouble in the bud. That might mean addressing two co-workers at the first hint of inappropriate friction between them or confronting a direct report at the first sign of insubordination.

Monkeying Around

I worked in Venezuela for two years alongside career missionaries. One Sunday morning I was worshipping in the Bethel Baptist Church in Caracas. In the middle of the service a monkey walked in through the back door. Even though this was downtown in a city of 4 million people, the man who lived next door to the church had a pet monkey and the monkey had gotten loose.

The monkey walked in and came up the aisle just as if he were a member who had arrived late, taking his seat in the second row. I don't remember what the congregation was doing at the time but the pastor might as well have announced, "Let's quit and watch the monkey," because that's what everyone was doing anyway. Everybody got a kick out of it, especially the kids.

In fact, the monkey was sitting behind three little boys and he leaned forward in his seat and began to pick at them. The monkey was out of line; he was disruptive and was abusing the boys in his monkey-like way. Of course the boys thought it was great; this was the most fun they'd ever had in church! Not one of the adults moved to rein in the monkey; we let him do his thing without consequence. We knew the monkey was acting inappropriately, but we just sat there and let him, well, monkey around.

It was actually amusing until the monkey got too rough and scratched a little boy hard enough to draw a little blood. The little boy began to cry, his parents got upset, and all of a sudden a molehill became a mountain. Getting rid of the monkey became our focus. Immediately people began to worry about rabies and to look for someone to blame. *How come nobody intervened to stop the monkey?* we all were asking ourselves after the service.

The moral of the story is that when the monkey starts getting out of hand—disrupting the organization and abusing those around him—the monkey must be dealt with.

Early on.

That does not mean we should jump immediately into a fray. As leaders we need to take a step back before charging in to set everyone and everything straight. Yet we can't become too tentative. Before things get out of hand, disruptive behavior must be addressed.

Just for Vocational Ministers

A leader's fear of hurting one person can sometimes lead to a number of others being hurt. We must stop divisive action before it spreads.

I know many people feel they never could exercise church discipline. "After all, what about grace?" some will protest. Others will say, "I'm not spiritual enough to judge someone else." Both comments raise important issues, but the fact remains that the Bible requires some type of discipline against those whose behavior threatens the well-being of the body of Christ (1 Corinthians 5:11; 2 Thessalonians 3:6,14; Titus 3:10,11).

Additionally, Paul writes, "Make every effort to keep the unity of the Spirit" (Ephesians 4:3). "Make every effort" is a verb of urgency. It means, "endeavor, struggle, strive." In some instances, that "endeavor" means dealing with divisive people in the faith community. And, in general, it is the pastor who will have to take the initiative in dealing with divisive people.

Bill Easum wrote "On Not Being Nice, 'For the Sake of the Gospel,'" a widely read and quoted article on church leadership, published in *Net Results*, April 1997. It is an article that every leader whose church is threatened by an intimidator must read. Easum begins his article by noting, "Throughout all of my consulting ministry, I have seen a disturbing pattern…most established churches are held hostage by one or two bullies." He goes on to say that many leaders are sacrificing the health of the churches they lead, all in the name of being nice. So let's not be too "nice"—our churches deserve more from us.

19

When People Disqualify Themselves

Players never get thrown out of a game. They disqualify themselves.

According to high school rules, if a player fights, intentionally contacts an official, or commits a flagrant foul, he has disqualified himself and is no longer allowed to participate in the game. By removing him from the action, the official is simply enforcing the rule. An official does not enforce disqualification lightly; it's always a tough call.

Disqualification is costly to the player. It's costly to the team. It's costly to the official. The coach might just protest the ejection. It might become necessary for the supervisor of officials to meet with school administrators. Film will be reviewed. The official's decision will come under heavy scrutiny. And if the official ejects too many players too often, he might be, as officials like to say, "the best non-working official in the country."

The official understands the cost to everyone when he determines that a player has forfeited his right to play. But it is not a decision that the official should be ashamed or hesitant to make.

Getting the Wrong Folks Off the Bus

Sometimes leaders will also conclude that certain persons within the organization have disqualified themselves. The many reasons could include harassment, shoddy work, moral failures, or incompetence. Sometimes organizations increase in complexity and people disqualify themselves by not engaging in ongoing personal development; the organization outgrows them. And sometimes the person's presence is simply like a pebble in the organization's shoe; his or her demeanor is so obviously disruptive that something has to be done.

Reassignment within the organization may be a viable solution; maybe the employee just needs a new role—a better "fit"—or maybe he or she simply needs a fresh start. Yet reassignment often feels like rearranging the deck chairs on the *Titanic*. When, for the sake of the organization and its mission, it is time for someone to go, the leader has to be courageous enough to say so.

In *Good to Great*, Jim Collins offers the now well-known analogy of the bus. You've got to get the right folks on the bus, he says, and you have to make sure they are in the right places. That's not all, however; you've also got to get the *wrong* folks *off* the bus. Good leaders always have known that removing incompetent, disruptive, or slothful people is one of their responsibilities.

The late Vince Lombardi's philosophy for football training camp was simple: "Weed out the uncommitted and get the last 10 percent out of everyone else." In *What It Takes To Be*

#1, Vince Lombardi, Jr., son of the legendary Packers coach, recounts his father's first day with the team. Coach Lombardi told his players:

> "I am going to find 36 men who have the pride to make any sacrifice to win. There are such men. If they're not here, I'll get them. If you are not one, if you don't want to play, you might as well leave right now."

National Hockey League Coach John Tortorella knows how difficult it is to terminate players—especially popular ones. When Tortorella released players who were fan favorites, he was publicly roasted. Fans hated him and even hung him in effigy. But cutting players the coach didn't think would produce was the right thing, no matter how hot things got. Tortorella describes what it's like to make unpopular personnel decisions:

> "You've got to . . . ask yourself, 'Is this the way it should be done for the best of the team?' And if you answer the question 'Yes' then you need to go with it. All decisions should be made for what's best for the hockey team...And you could lose your job over that. But you still can't bend and try to please everybody."
> —Christian Klemash, *How to Succeed in the Game of Life*

I'm not advocating a hard-hearted, bottom-line-only approach to spiritual leadership, yet we have to insist on top performances from those we supervise. A failure to be tough when a subordinate's performance is unacceptable is a disservice both to the organization and to that subordinate. A strong aversion to confrontation makes for a poor supervisor.

Steps to Termination

I like Jack Welch's perspective on the tough call to terminate a staff member. In *Jack*, the former chairman and CEO of General Electric writes: "Removing people will always be the hardest decision a leader faces. Anyone who 'enjoys doing it' shouldn't be on the payroll, and neither should anyone who 'can't do it.'"

If you are a leader, you are going to have to be willing to fire people.

Sometimes people egregiously violate the rules. They steal from the company or do something outrageous that requires immediate dismissal. But usually the problem is less clear-cut and requires a step-by-step process before termination.

The process that precedes termination is critical, and as Christ-followers we must be sure to be completely fair in this regard. The process begins with assessing whether the employee has been adequately equipped for the job he or she is being asked to do. Training is certainly less painful than termination for the employee and more economical for the organization.

If it can be determined that training is not the problem, the process should continue. The employee should be notified plainly that his or her performance is unsatisfactory, and specific, measurable goals for improvement should be provided in writing. There should be specified means of evaluating progress toward those goals and clearly stated consequences should be delineated should those goals not be met. If satisfactory progress is not achieved in a timely manner, then further steps toward termination become necessary.

Fairness is the key here. Just remember that fairness is as important for the organization as for the individual. It is unfair to the organization for its leaders to accept unproductive or disruptive conduct from employees. The primary responsibility of the leader, in fact, is the overall health and effectiveness of the organization.

Of course the need to terminate someone often reflects poorly on the leader. It might be that the leader either didn't hire well or didn't coach well. If either is true, then the situation can be considered a failure of leadership.

It is critical that we think through the repercussions of our decision before we release someone. This is one of those leadership calls that is best made only after getting wise counsel. The individual to be dismissed and his or her family will suffer because of our decision, and that decision must not be made carelessly. And, in our litigious society, it is prudent to get legal advice before terminating an employee.

Above all, we have a Christian responsibility to look out for the one we are terminating. When appropriate, and being careful not to mislead potential employers, we can help the person find a new place of service. Obviously, a terminated employee can forfeit our help if he or she reacts inappropriately to the dismissal. Yet, as much as lies with us, we must do our best to be gracious and to attempt to make the parting of ways as amicable and as mutually beneficial as possible.

Even Volunteers Can Be Fired

As I've said earlier, I often work as the head linesman on the officiating crew, which means I am responsible for the yard-to-gain markers and the down box, the piece of equipment that displays the number of the down. The volunteers who handle those markers are called the chain crew. They receive no compensation for helping me, so I deeply appreciate them and express my sincere gratitude before and after the game.

Nevertheless, there are guidelines they have to follow. They can't coach or cheer, and they can't try to officiate. I don't mind a casual questioning of our crew's calls from time to time, but caustic criticism is not acceptable.

One of the best games I ever officiated was tainted by the attitude of one of my chain crew members. He had ridiculed our calls far too often and far too caustically. So, I finally said to him, "You're gonna have to knock off the comments. Just keep the chains and let us officiate."

"You can always fire me," he audaciously declared, as if I'd never consider such a thing.

"I might do that," I answered, without flinching.

I was silently grateful that he kept his comments to himself after that. Yet the truth is, if the situation gets bad enough, I can fire a volunteer chain crew member.

Some of you lead organizations that rely heavily on volunteers. Maybe it's a large nonprofit organization or a homeless shelter. Maybe it's a local hospice or a Red Cross chapter or the elementary school PTA. Just because people have volunteered doesn't mean they shouldn't be held to a high standard. We cannot accept sloppy work, minimal commitment, or even disruptive behavior. When we do that, we aren't doing them any favors, and we're hurting the organization.

We owe volunteers and all who work with us the best training available. When we provide high-quality training opportunities, we communicate that we value their work. We also owe volunteers the kind of appreciation that will let them know we don't take them for granted. Furthermore, we owe it to them to hold them to a high standard. We insult people when we expect too little of them. That means volunteers can be fired.

The High Road Can Be Lonely

A good leader never will be lonelier than when he or she makes the tough call to release someone. Even if he or she has sought good counsel, weighed the consequences carefully, checked his or her motives, followed due process, and has a justifiable cause for termination, the leader is still likely to be perceived negatively by some. No matter the reason for dismissal, it is likely the one who was released has friends remaining within the organization, and those allies probably will feel the leader has mistreated their friend.

In such a situation, the leader would like nothing more than to reveal the whole story about the one who has been terminated. If all could be told, folks might not question the wisdom of dismissing that person. People might even wonder why the leader took so long to do so. Yet the leader is probably going to have to suffer the criticism in silence, for he or she is bound to the high road.

And the high road can get awfully lonesome.

Just for Vocational Ministers

Of course, churches and Christian organizations face unique issues when considering terminating an employee. For that reason, this section is a bit longer than unusual.

A senior pastor must never allow a handful of disgruntled members to run off a good staff minister. Yet, there are times when a staff minister does need to be released. That's a tough call for a number of reasons.

First, in a church, vocational ministers develop a following. The termination of a staff member could give rise to a real PR problem. (Reread the section about Coach Tortorella earlier in this chapter.) The cost—and it could be considerable—must be counted when mulling over a decision to terminate a staff member whom many believe hung the moon. If church members never have seen the side of the minster that you see, they may be blindsided—and upset—by his or her termination.

Second, in a church that follows a congregational form of government (in other words, when ultimate authority rests with the congregation, not the senior pastor, a board, or a bishop), there is accountability to the entire congregation for the way personnel matters are handled. A pastor, for example, could soon be joining his former colleague in the unemployment line if it is perceived that he dismissed a staff member without justifiable cause.

And third, it is difficult to dismiss a friend and colleague. It's tough to terminate someone with whom you have prayed, performed funerals, and led worship.

Nevertheless, the right thing is the right thing. Leadership requires making the hard calls, and sometimes dismissal, handled fairly and compassionately, is the right thing even when the consequences are painful. When people disqualify themselves by poor performance or some other unacceptable conduct, we do a disservice to the kingdom of God by not letting them go.

In *When Moses Meets Aaron: Staffing and Supervision in Large Congregations*, by Gil Rendle and Susan Beaumont, there is a chapter titled, "Dealing with Poor Performance or Terminating Employment." There the authors present five steps of "progressive discipline": (1) the verbal warning; (2) the written warning; (3) the final warning; (4) the termination; and (5) the resignation agreement and general release. Every staff leader needs to keep that chapter handy, no matter the size of the staff. Of particular interest to me was the section in the book on how to communicate a staff termination to the congregation. We have to assure the church family that the process was fair and involved trusted leaders, without sharing unnecessary information. We have to know the difference between "maintaining confidentiality and keeping a secret."

No Volunteers-for-Life

Greg Hunt, a fellow pastor, has helped me consider the nature of accountability for volunteers within a church. He makes a critical distinction between a person and a position. A *person's* worth is unconditional, and we have value to one another A *position* is one's role in the church, and while one's value is unconditional, one's position is not. Positions depend on performance and the circumstances within an organization.

Hunt's observations remind us that an individual's value is not dependent upon the position he or she holds. While this way of thinking does not eliminate the possibility of conflict, it should maximize the potential for objectivity and minimize the potential for broken relationships.

If volunteers are not performing well, be sure that they get the best training possible. Be sure to encourage them as well so that their morale is high. Yet, if they still don't do their job properly, find a way to let them know that no position is permanent.

For example, in one of my previous pastorates there was a difficult situation with a children's Sunday School teacher. She had been teaching for decades, but had grown terribly impatient. It had gotten so that she was terrorizing the kids. Some faithful parents had said they would not bring their children to Sunday School while she was their teacher, and I didn't blame them.

A church leader and I met with this teacher more than once, explaining our concerns. Nothing changed.

Finally we met with her and spoke kindly but frankly. We expressed our appreciation for her service over the years and asked her to step down. She didn't take it very well, but ultimately she resigned. Actually it turned out better than I'd expected. Another teacher stepped in, the children returned, and all ended well.

I'm sure the long-time teacher was offended, but offending her was a reasonable price to pay for the health of our congregation. I announced to church leaders what had happened, just in case they heard a complaint. Their only response: "This should have happened a long time ago."

SECTION SIX
MORE PEOPLE ISSUES

*Not many of you should presume to
be teachers, my brothers, because you
know that we who teach will be judged
more strictly.*
—James 3:1

20

There's a Time
and a Place

I remember a look I got from a fellow official during a playoff game. I had not positioned myself well to make a call. The slip-up was not obvious. It didn't affect the play. And the coaches, players, and fans were not aware of it. The other official, however, saw me out of position.

Because he didn't want to damage my credibility, he didn't call attention to my error in such a way that anyone else could see. I got the message, though, when he gave me a sly, but clear look that said, "You really messed up that one."

Sometimes leaders mess up. And sometimes people within an organization have serious and legitimate disagreements. But in any case, the leader must insist that reprimands and disagreements be limited to the appropriate contexts. It baffles me, for example, when the coach of a professional sports team allows a player to trash his teammates in the media. There is a place, such as in the coach's office or in team meetings, for candid conversations. But nothing good comes from public disputes.

An Ugly Scene

Ned Wilford was officiating a great college football rivalry—Florida and Florida State. The officiating crew was mixed, with some from the Southeastern Conference (SEC) and some from the Independent Officials Association. At the time, Florida State was an independent; Florida was, and is, an SEC team.

In *You Threw the Flag, You Make the Call*, Wilford says that it was in this game that he witnessed the only incident of shady officiating during his long career. One of the independent officials had a beef with the SEC, and, at a critical point in the game, he tried to give an advantage to Florida State. The official in question threw a flag against Florida for no reason, just to offset a flag thrown by Wilford against Florida State, Wilford writes. That official's flagrant favoritism, and the incongruity among the crew, publicly embarrassed Wilford and the other officials who were trying to get things right.

Wilford follows up his story with this application for leaders and executive teams:

> *You may have part of your executive team that does not agree with your solution to a problem or the solutions of some other team members. Differences of opinion are fine and will inevitably occur. But, you don't want to be going into a board meeting with recommendations for major policy issues and changes, and then have one of your peers start second-guessing or criticizing a decision that has already been made. The difference should be voiced and resolved before the board meeting; once a final, group decision has been made, the members of the group must*

cover each others' flags. You must support the group,
especially in a public environment.

. . . There can be plenty of free and open conflict in coming to
a consensus, but once there is tacit agreement in words and
actions that the decision is agreed upon, the time for crossing
someone else's call in a public setting is absolutely over.

Our church staff engages in periodic strategy talks during which everyone is encouraged to speak candidly about any concerns. We try to "push" until we feel no one is withholding something they want to say about issues that matter. Sometimes those discussions are tough, but tough discussions are required of effective teams.

The expectation, however, is that we say what we need to say in the context of that meeting, not behind a fellow staffer's back in the presence of people outside the staff. It is also expected that staff members won't criticize or disagree with a team decision once the discussion moves outside the room. If a discussion takes place after our staff meeting that reveals new and useful information, a staff member is free to say, "Let me take this to the staff one more time." He or she is not free, however, to jump to the other side of the fence and contradict the team's decision.

We are trying hard to practice the principle that in private we can have frank and uncomfortable discussions, but in public we are a team.

Honoring Each Other

I have told the church staff that the door is always open for them to differ with me, but not in front of members of the congregation. I don't expect staff members to violate their values in order to support me. However, the health of the church is in jeopardy if staff members criticize me to church members. Furthermore, staff members know that if someone tries to draw them into a triangle by disparaging me, they are to say, "You need to talk to Travis." No leader can allow dissension and negativity to ferment behind his or her back.

No one should be a yes-person, and the right to disagree honorably is understood. Yet disagreements with a leader's decisions and objections to his or her leadership in particular projects should not be shared publicly. Moreover, if someone has fundamental problems with the values and vision of the leader, he or she is not going to be happy in that place of service.

Of course, sometimes a church staff member and I might agree that in an upcoming meeting we would openly acknowledge disagreement. It is not necessarily destructive for a staff member to say in a public forum, "The leader and I disagree on this matter." Yet that kind of a public statement should be agreed upon beforehand. No leader should ever be blindsided by open opposition.

It is important also to understand that members of our church staff can expect the same loyalty from me that I insist on from them. If someone comes to me with a complaint about the staff, I won't join in a berate-fest. If the complaint has any merit, it is my responsibility to follow up directly with that staff member, or at least with his or her supervisor. I will not, however, dishonor that staff member by vilifying him or her among people outside our staff circle. In private we might have frank and uncomfortable discussions, but in public we are united.

Just for Vocational Ministers

Not so long ago, the day before a meeting in which several of us were going to discuss a strategic issue, one of the staff members came into my office. "I think you and I ought to talk about this today," he said, "because I don't want to be on the opposite side of the table from you tomorrow."

That was a mature thing for him to do. He did need to speak freely; yet in the upcoming meeting, with people from outside the staff present, it would indeed have been unhealthy for our church to have the two of us engage in open disagreement. By meeting with me privately he got the opportunity to get his issues on the table, and his insights became part of the equation without it having to look like he and I were pulling in different directions. It would be equally important had *I* known that we were in disagreement about something to talk with him beforehand.

21

Who's in
Charge Here?

When the officiating crew and I walk out on the field at
the beginning of a game, most folks don't understand
our distinct roles. They call us all "referees" (and sometimes
a few other names).

The truth is, though, that only one of us is the referee.
(Others on the crew have different titles—back judge, umpire,
head linesman, etc.) Any of us can call a penalty, and each
member of the crew has a voice when there is a disputed matter.
When push comes to shove, however, the man with the final
say-so is the man in the white hat—the *real* referee. When in
doubt about a decision, we all look to the referee. We don't poll
the fans or survey the coaching staffs; the referee makes the
call. Rule 1, Section 1, Article 6 of the National Federation of
High Schools football rulebook reads, "The referee's decisions
are final in all matters pertaining to the game."

A discussion by the entire officiating crew is most often
the appropriate approach to a decision. And sometimes, when
certain members of the crew have more experience than he

does, the referee will get some extra help on tough calls from them. I've started "refereeing" some lately, and often there will be an official or two on the field who is more knowledgeable than me. Usually I will check quickly with them before making my official ruling and/or administering a complex penalty. Yet if I'm wearing the white hat for that game, I cannot abdicate my responsibility as head of the crew. There must be a person in charge, a person to look to when a clear voice is needed. Such is the role of the referee...and the leader.

The Captain of the Ship

Teamwork gurus talk about everybody having a say-so in decision making. We are told that everyone should feel like they have ownership in their organization's decisions. I get that. But I also know that when the rubber hits the road *someone* has to be in charge.

Of course, heavy-handed, bureaucratic administration went out with leisure suits. "Team" has replaced the corporate food chain. Conventional wisdom has it that in today's postmodern culture we need participatory leadership. I'm not advocating a return to outdated styles and structures. But I am in agreement with the unequivocal declaration of management guru Peter Drucker:

> *One hears a great deal today about "the end of hierarchy." This is blatant nonsense. In any institution there has to be a final authority, that is, a "boss"—someone who can make the final decision . . . If the ship founders, the captain does not call a meeting, the captain gives an order . . . Hierarchy, and the unquestioning acceptance*

TOUGH CALLS

of it by everyone in the organization, is the only hope in a crisis.

—"Management's New Paradigms," *Forbes*,
   October 5, 1998

Of course, every situation is not a crisis. A team discussion is most often the appropriate approach to a decision. Yet, there must be a captain. In certain circumstances, the leader must be able to count on his or her associates to follow a directive.

If you are the "referee"—the final authority—then do not abdicate your role. Be decisive. Don't expect someone else to make the call. If you are the leader, then *lead* for goodness' sake!

From the Ref's Perspective

There are aspects of the referee position that I could not have understood before I actually began to step into that role. As the head linesman, I am responsible for my position and my area of the field. As the referee, however, I am accountable for the entire game. As the head linesman, if another member of the crew makes a mistake the impact on me is minimal. As the referee, however, I feel a personal responsibility for the performance of other crew members.

Similarly, if you are not the one in a position of final authority, then you don't know what it's like to walk in those shoes. You can, however, try to appreciate the position of the one who *is*. Quite frankly, the load of the top leader can get pretty heavy, and his or her life can get pretty lonely. Furthermore, chances are that he or she is looking at situations from a much wider perspective than yours, which includes details of which you're not aware.

When we lived in Nigeria our sending agency came up with some strategies with which we and many of our fellow missionaries in Nigeria did not agree. I don't remember the details now; I just remember that we didn't like the folks in Richmond (the home office) telling us how to do our work in Nigeria. We understood our context and felt like we knew what to do better than someone an ocean away.

We had a valid point. However, now I understand the situation a bit differently. The people in Richmond had the entire world in view. We in Nigeria had only *our corner* of the world in view.

So, if you are not the "referee," recognize the senior leader's responsibility. Remember that the person at the helm has to consider the health and effectiveness of the entire organization, and he or she might be the only person who keeps the total operation in view. His or her attempt to balance the many viable (and sometimes competing) programs and interests in the organization is a bit like spinning various plates while walking a tightrope over the Grand Canyon.

The One to Make the Tough Calls

Teamwork and strong leadership are not mutually exclusive. A good leader will encourage vigorous discussion about important issues and let the corporate wisdom shape the decision making. Senior leaders should do their best to involve everyone in the process of making tough calls. In the end, however, Coach Wooden is right: "When a decision is made, it must be accepted by those on your team, or they must be encouraged to find another team" (from *Wooden on Leadership*, with Steve Jamison).

Of course the people on the team can disagree with the leader during the decision-making process. And they can even disagree with the leader privately after a decision has been made. However, if they cannot genuinely respect the leader's decisions, then it may best for them to seek another team or organization.

I'm not at all suggesting that senior leaders be dictatorial. Nonetheless, people are going to look primarily to one leader, not a *team* of leaders, to make the calls—especially the tough ones.

Just for Vocational Ministers

There is a sense among some that the day of the one-pastor-church may be over. In his excellent book, *The Great Giveaway*, David E. Fitch suggests:

> *One possible way to avoid the CEO-pastor syndrome is to institute multiple recognized leadership in the church pastorate . . . [P]erhaps there should be no senior pastor at all. Rather, multiple co-pastors may act as a college of leadership for each church . . . There should never be one superman (or superwoman) pastor.*

That is an intriguing concept, and I deeply appreciate the spirit behind it. I would agree that the "CEO-pastor syndrome" and "superpastors" are symptomatic of our

---

departure from the biblical model of the shepherd. The church should heed Fitch's warning about Lone Ranger luminaries with the title of pastor. And I do know of a few wonderful congregations in which there is a team of pastors with specific responsibilities that match their specific gifts. Yet I cannot believe that the norm ever should be anything except one primary pastor for a congregation.

I don't believe the church needs leadership clusters. I believe we need pastors who take seriously this complicated role of shepherd-overseer.

22

Leading Without the White Hat

It was high drama. The home team was losing by less than six points, and they had the ball with time running out. I counted the offensive players. I counted 11 of them, which is a good thing, because there are *supposed* to be 11. The ball was snapped, and on an impressive pass play the home team scored and the home crowd went wild...

Until they saw the yellow flag in the backfield.

The referee (the only guy in the white hat) turned toward the press box and signaled illegal participation. He'd counted 12 men on offense. I stepped toward him and indicated that I'd counted 11, but he was certain about his call and stuck with it.

The touchdown was nullified by the penalty, and the ball was brought back behind where it had been snapped previously. Two scoreless plays later the clock hit 0:00 and the visiting team celebrated. The home team coach was somewhat less than appreciative of the penalty that cost him a touchdown, and he felt free to express that.

I'm not quite certain that there were more than 11 men on the offensive side of the ball, and I was surprised the referee didn't recognize the problem (if there *was* a problem) before the play went off. I was frustrated. Yet, despite my frustration, the referee (who has been officiating a lot longer than I have) counted 12, and the referee gets the final word. Though I had input, I was in a role of secondary leadership.

Second-Chair Leaders

There are many positions of secondary leadership:

- The official who is part of the crew but not the referee.
- The defensive coach who has to follow the overall vision of the head coach but who also has to inject his personal philosophy of defense.
- The assistant foreman on the night shift who mentors the workers on the floor, while the senior foreman gets the credit for the workers' outstanding production.
- The assistant regional manager to whom everyone goes for answers and results (instead of to the regional manager).
- The executive assistant to the vice-president who is the calming presence in a division of the company that always seems to have a storm brewing.
- The assistant principal whose knowledge of the school's inner workings makes her the go-to person.

Mike Bonem and Roger Patterson discuss such leaders in their book, *Leading From the Second Chair*. They define a second-chair leader as "a person in a subordinate role whose influence with others adds value throughout the organization." The second-chair leader has to be able to find joy in helping *others* achieve their dreams; an envious person will be miserable in the second chair. The mission of the organization must be that which energizes the person in secondary leadership, for the spotlight usually will be on someone else. Team accomplishments have to be more important than individual accolades.

Those in second-chair leadership must maintain a positive attitude toward, and a healthy relationship with, the senior leader. The goal is loyalty without acquiescence. The rewards tend to be less public than the rewards of the senior leader, and if the second-chair leader can be content with that, then there can be great satisfaction in leading without being the buck-stopper.

Second-chair leaders have to perform a balancing act. They must balance their desire to lead with their need to submit to the overall vision of the organization. Second-chair leaders have to keep the big picture in view while championing their particular areas of responsibility and passion.

Working Under Imperfect Leaders

Some of you work under great senior leaders. For you, leading from the second chair simply means exerting valuable influence, being a catalyst for progress, and facilitating positive change, all without having the title of "Big Cheese." Yet every leader makes mistakes, and unless you are at the very top of your organization, you are going to have to follow imperfect people.

Of course, it is a unique challenge to follow a leader who constantly makes poor decisions or, worse, one who is unethical or immoral. Obviously, one answer is to find a spot in another organization, but that might not be the right answer for you. If you do decide to remain as a second-chair leader where the one in charge is not offering good leadership, then you are going to have to be patient and wise.

You are going to have to defer when deference is difficult, to grant authority when you feel authority is not merited, and to remain true to your moral compass without being sanctimoniously insubordinate. You will have to look for ways to accentuate the strengths of that leader and to question him or her in appropriate ways when he or she is blind to a potential problem.

If you cannot in good conscience follow the leadership of the one to whom you report, then you owe it to the organization, to yourself, and even to the leader, to find another place of service. If you are going to remain, then you have to follow that leader.

Many of you will decide to remain where you are, despite your leader's weaknesses. Perhaps you will stay because the organization is so wonderful, or because you love your role there. Perhaps the leader, though imperfect, is stretching you in painful, yet valuable, ways. Perhaps you simply don't want to put your kids through another move. Whatever your reason for staying, I encourage you to honor your leader when you can and to remember that he or she almost certainly has more on his or her plate than you know about.

Following Effectively

One of the most helpful resources I have seen regarding second-chair leaders is Robert Kelley's popular article "In Praise of Followers," published in the *Harvard Business Review*, November-December 1988. Kelley notes that in our preoccupation with effective leadership we have forgotten the importance of effective followership. Followership does not have to be a sheep-like, zombie-like, mindless acquiescence to the boss's commands. Effective followership, according to Kelley, is "enthusiastic, intelligent, and self-reliant participation—without star billing—in the pursuit of an organizational goal." Some choose to exercise their gifts in roles without the grand titles and can make a significant contribution to their organizations.

Kelley proposes the following as the qualities of effective followers:

1. **"They manage themselves well."** Effective followers need minimal supervision. They understand lines of responsibility, yet they see themselves as co-laborers with the top leadership. They exercise their power of influence judiciously and are not afraid to disagree with the chain of command in appropriate ways.

2. **"They are committed to the organization and to a purpose, principle, or person outside themselves."** Personal success and organizational achievements are one and the same. This kind of commitment is inspirational and contagious.

3. **"They build their competence and focus their efforts for maximum impact."** Effective followers

don't have to be told to seek opportunities for personal and professional development. Their personal standard of excellence is higher than that which the organization requires of them, and they are always on the lookout for ways to maximize the performance of the organization.

4. "They are courageous, honest, and credible." Their courage, honesty, and credibility allow them to speak up in appropriate ways when the emperor has no clothes. They hold themselves and the organization to high standards and keep the first-chair leaders on their toes.

Kelley continues:

> *People who are effective in the follower role have the vision to see both the forest and the trees, the social capacity to work well with others, the strength of character to flourish without heroic status, the moral and psychological balance to pursue personal and corporate goals at no cost to either, and, above all, the desire to participate in a team effort for the accomplishment of some greater common purpose.*
>
> —"In Praise of Followers," *Harvard Business Review*, November-December 1988

Just for Vocational Ministers

I highly recommend the book *Leading From the Second Chair* by Mike Bonem and Roger Patterson. The book was written particularly for those who serve on a church staff but are not senior pastors. We reviewed the key principles from that book on a recent staff retreat and it was helpful for all of us to look at each other's roles from the other side.

If you are not the senior pastor I want to encourage you. Your ability to lead, often behind-the-scenes, is both admirable and essential for the life and health of your church. God bless all the Joshuas who serve down in the valley while the Moseses stand up on the hill.

23

Stress on the Family

Don Denkinger was an outstanding Major League Baseball umpire. Unfortunately, he is best known for making an honest, but glaring mistake in the 1985 World Series. The St. Louis Cardinals were up three games to two and ahead 1–0 in the ninth inning of the sixth and potentially final game of the Series. When Denkinger incorrectly called the Kansas City Royals' Jorge Orta safe at first, the Royals took advantage of the break and went on to score the tying and winning runs later in the ninth inning. That forced a seventh game, and in that game Kansas City beat St. Louis, denying the Cardinals the glory that had been so close. Although the Cardinals had blown several opportunities to put the Royals away in that sixth game, Denkinger was viciously blamed for the loss.

Dave Phillips, a fellow umpire, was watching that sixth game on television at a wedding reception. He recounts what happened next in his book, *Center Field on Fire*, with Rob Rains. When he saw Don Denkinger miss the call, Phillips anticipated that things would get ugly. Though he felt badly for his fellow umpire, Phillips' first thoughts were of Denkinger's family. He knew they would be watching and hearing the vitriolic criticism of Don, so Phillips called their home.

One of Denkinger's daughters answered, and she was weeping. When Phillips introduced himself, the daughter cried, "They are being so mean to my dad!" Don's wife got on the phone and reported that she'd already begun receiving unbelievably threatening phone calls from irate St. Louis fans.

Shoot Him!

Earl Strom tells a similar but lighter story in *Calling the Shots* about taking his young daughters to watch him officiate an NBA game. He figured his little girls would be safe with the "three heavyset women" who always sat underneath the basket. The three ladies agreed to watch Strom's girls.

Near the end of the second quarter, Strom twisted his ankle and hit the floor. While a trainer tended to his ankle, fans began to yell, "Shoot him! They shoot horses, why not referees!" And do you know who was yelling the loudest? Those three women watching Strom's daughters!

A few minutes later, at the half, Strom limped into the locker room and was followed by his weeping daughters. "What's wrong?" Strom asked his little girls when he saw their big, teary eyes. "Daddy, they're not going to shoot you, are they?" his daughters wanted to know.

It can be difficult for officials' families. I've experienced it myself. As I write this, our 17-year-old son, Grant, is in his second year of umpiring Little League baseball (and is a fine umpire, I might add). Sometimes I watch him work a game without anyone knowing I'm the umpire's father. And a couple of times I've wanted to say, "Hey, that's my boy you're talking about!"

At times, the families of leaders (like the families of officials) overhear venomous words about their loved ones. "Shoot him" is not the worst that has been said of some of us. Hearing malicious criticisms is painful for family members. And, on occasion, the family members themselves can become the objects of attack. That's when nasty people really have crossed the line.

Protecting Your Loved Ones

In Fall 2004 *Leadership* magazine ran an article titled "Navigational Errors." In the article, the author (whose name was withheld) made the following observation:

> A fireman cannot tell the fire chief, "I'm not going to enter that burning building and rescue those people because, well, it's a risk, and my wife and my kids lose sleep when they know I'm on the job." The captain of a sinking ship doesn't jump into the first lifeboat because he has a family to think about.
>
> There are some jobs—and they tend to be the most vital in a community—in which pressure, worry, gossip, and rejection are felt not just by the person but also by his family.

The author is right; pressure on the family comes with the leadership territory. On the other hand, there obviously are limits to the abuse to which a spiritual leader should expose his or her family.

What about the little boy who overhears teachers complain about his mom, the school principal? What about the lady in the stands who hears fans belittle her husband, the coach? What about the wife of the mayor who sees her beloved husband maligned in the media? What about the daughter of the executive who sees her mother weep after an acrimonious board meeting? Sometimes it hurts to love a leader.

The late Tom Gorman, an MLB umpire, described for author Lee Gutkind how his wife, who regularly attended his games, used to react to thoughtless fans:

> *"Whenever anyone in the stands would boo me, or in some way criticize my work on the field, she'd jump all over them, holler and scream and threaten all kinds of legal action until they'd apologize."*
> —*The Best Seat in Baseball, But You Have to Stand*

I'm sure the spouses and families of countless leaders would like very much to "jump all over" their loved one's detractors and would love to "holler and scream and threaten all kinds of legal action." Yet the Christian family is expected to keep quiet and let God handle the retribution. That is often a difficult and painful thing.

So what are leaders to do about their families, especially their children? It's a tough call. On the one hand, the children of leaders can watch their parents and learn important lessons about in-the-middle-of-difficulties character. They can learn lessons that prepare them for the real world that awaits them should they choose to lead some day. Yet parents will have to decide if those lessons are coming at too great a cost. I believe that decision depends largely on the *issues*, the *organization*, and the *personalities* of the children.

First, are the *issues* of such substance and import that they outweigh the sacrifices of the family? Second, is the *organization* of such value to the world, and the attitude of its people so inspiring, that the sacrifice does not seem wasted? Third, just how deeply are the kids being affected? That will depend largely on the *personalities* and makeup, or temperament, of the children. I can't think of anything worth destroying the sons and daughters whom God has entrusted to the care of those of us who are parents.

Just for Vocational Ministers

I remember the day I was being voted on by the First Baptist Church of Mt. Washington, Kentucky. Members of the search committee sat with our family in the church fellowship hall while we waited to see if the church would call me as their pastor.

When the church moderator stepped into the room he had a smile on his face. There had been only four negative votes out of the entire congregation. There were hugs and handshakes all around. We all were thrilled.

Except for Brennan, our nine-year-old daughter. Brennan was concerned, and that night she expressed her concern. "Why would four people vote against you, Daddy?" she asked so sincerely. At that tender age, she

---

TOUGH CALLS

couldn't understand why anyone would vote against Dad.

What if she had heard people say I am not worthy of being called a "pastor," not earning my salary, or that I ought to be run out of town? That would have been devastating. Yet that is exactly the kind of thing that children sometimes overhear about their minister-parents. Parents have a responsibility to protect their family from exposure to that kind of unchristian behavior.

Of course vocational ministers who are also parents have a responsibility to be careful what they say in front of the kids. Unfortunately, the sons and daughters of ministers sometimes sit at the dinner table and hear their mom and dad criticize the congregation—everybody from the kitchen committee to the clerk to the captain of the church softball team. That is terribly unhealthy.

Commiserating about the behavior of church members, even when commiserating is justified, ought to take place behind closed doors. Yet parents cannot completely shield their sons and daughters from cruel comments by insensitive critics. When those critics get too personal, ministers and their spouses have a tough call to make. Do they stay and fight because the mission of the church is that important, or do they resign and slip away so that their kids won't be subjected to the kind of malice that some church members, unfortunately, can unleash?

G. Lloyd Rediger wrote the book, Clergy Killers, and spent a whole chapter dealing with "collateral damage"—the pain inflicted on the spouses and children of pastors under attack. Some churches, in my opinion, are not worth subjecting a family to such anguish. There are churches, quite frankly, that have become habitual minister-bashers. Even the decent folks of those churches don't deserve to have the minister stay and fight, for the decent ones have stood by and let the tyrants take over.

Other churches, however, are worth a fight. These churches have a good track record and great potential. They are temporarily being held hostage by mean-spirited people, but will bounce back and again become effective communities of faith if they are given strong leadership.

Fight or flight? It's a tough call. And I'd say it depends on the church.

Section Seven
A Mind-Set

*Finally, brothers, whatever is true,
whatever is noble, whatever is right,
whatever is pure, whatever is lovely,
whatever is admirable—if anything is
excellent or praiseworthy—think about
such things.*
—Philippians 4:8

24

"My First Step Is Back"

My friend Bob Oldham and I took our sons to see the Washington Nationals play the Atlanta Braves in D.C. The husband and wife sitting beside us were nice enough, but they were season-ticket-holding, die-hard, opinionated Washington Nationals fans. Bob and I, and our sons, were pulling for the Braves.

Braves right fielder Brian Jordan hit a long ball down the left-field line. It could not have been more close to the foul line when it plopped over the fence. Was it fair or foul? Did it fall inside or outside that big, bright pole that determines the foul line? The third-base umpire called it a fair ball—a home run. Well, about 25,000 Washington Nationals fans went bananas. They jumped and screamed until another umpire, the crew chief, stepped in and overturned the call.

When the first umpire ruled it a home run, the man seated next to me immediately sprang to his feet (as if he thought the umpire would be able to see and hear him better). He yelled and screamed. "It was obviously a foul ball!" he protested.

I believe the guy next to me actually believed the ball was foul. But there were two problems. One, this gentleman was sitting about a quarter of a mile from where the speck of a ball dropped. Two, he is human, and he saw the conflict through biased eyes. He believed the ball was foul because he is like the rest of us; we all see things through our own lenses. (Television replays, by the way, showed that indeed it was a home run. The first umpire was right; the crew chief and the guy next to me were wrong.)

We all make judgments about people and situations from our own perspective—and we're often blind to the faults in ourselves. So it's important to remember Jesus's piercing words, "You hypocrite, first take the plank out of your own eye, and then you will see clearly to remove the speck from your brother's eye" (Matthew 7:5). When trouble erupts, it's especially important to take a moment to ask, "Am I seeing what I *think* I'm seeing?"

Take a Step Back

Not so long ago I was talking with one of our veteran back judges. That experienced official told me, "My first step is back."

"I can always step forward after the play begins," he said. "But if those receivers take off downfield I need to make sure they don't get behind me. So when the ball is snapped I step back and look at the action before I commit to going forward."

That's a great mind-set for leaders, especially when conflict breaks out. We need to take a step back and survey the situation. I admit that when trouble breaks out, my tendency is to rush in and start setting people straight. That's been called the ready-fire-aim approach. It's far better for me, however, when I back up before I rush in. If the action is headed toward me as a leader I need time to think—time to get my thoughts together before my mouth starts moving.

By stepping back we also give ourselves time to discern whether or not we own some responsibility for the problem. Before we start naming, blaming, and shaming, we must acknowledge whatever role *we* are playing in the conflict.

Quite candidly, probably all of us are hard to get along with at one time or another. Catch any of us at the wrong time and we can be rather surly. So when we are in conflict with someone, we need to ask ourselves:

Am I being completely honest with everyone involved or am I shading the truth in order to make people sympathetic to my cause?

Am I looking for a win/win situation or am I being stubborn and hard-headed?

Am I purely interested in doing what is right or am I merely intent on putting that person I don't like in his or her place?

What is it about me, or my personality, or my approach, that perhaps has made this situation worse?

When dealing with difficult people, it is helpful for me to remember a humbling experience I had when reading the book, *Don't Let Jerks Get the Best of You* by Paul Meier. I bought the book hoping it would help me handle blockheads and tyrants. Imagine my surprise when I took the book's "jerk test" and found that I have some jerky tendencies myself!

It is important to stand firmly against the manipulation and mutiny of difficult people. It is equally important that we not always assume that the difficult person is someone *else*.

Peace with All Men

Scripture instructs us, "Make every effort to live in peace with all men" (Hebrews 12:14). Romans 12:18 is even more explicit: "If it is possible, as far as it depends on you, live at peace with everyone." These words, inspired by God's Spirit, mean that I have a responsibility to do everything within my power to resolve conflict.

These verses of Scripture will not let me rationalize hateful thoughts, justify malicious actions, or explain away my offensive words. I must own my part of the dissension. I must face my flaws, swallow my pride, and go the extra mile to make sure there is a peaceful resolution to any fracas in which I am involved.

There will be occasions when we are blameless, and happen to be dealing with a cantankerous, contentious, quarrelsome person. That happens. But let's be honest enough to acknowledge any responsibility we have for the squabble at hand. We'll never be able to "make every effort to live at peace with all men" unless our first step is back.

Just for Vocational Ministers

The topic of this chapter requires a balancing act for most of us who are vocational ministers. We tend to dislike confrontation, and many of us step back *too far* when faced with potential conflict. It is indeed important that we step back long enough and far enough to see whether we are at fault and to get an accurate assessment of the situation. After a brief step backward, however, we must be willing to take action to right any wrong.

Step back. Just don't step so far back that you're out of the picture.

25

Kindness Goes
a Long Way

A sports official is not running for Mr. or Ms. Congeniality.
The goal of officiating is not to be considered "nice." Yet
an antagonistic attitude is not a prerequisite of authority. A
positive relationship with players and coaches goes a long way.
Retired NFL referee Jim Tunney shares this story:

> Jim Zorn was the first quarterback for the Seattle franchise.
> His mother, Esther, was the cafeteria manager for one of
> our schools when I was superintendent of the Bellflower
> United School District. One time she asked me to say hello
> for her when I worked a Seahawks game. I said I would.
> During the game Zorn, who was the Seahawks captain,
> had to elect a penalty option. I said, "Before I tell you
> what your options are, your mother says hello."
> —Jim Tunney with Glenn Dickey, *Impartial Judgment*

I've read that patients are much less likely to sue their doctors
if their doctors are friendly. Good bedside manner—an affable

personality—seems to provide greater protection against malpractice suits than skill does. In the same way, cultivating a friendly relationship with people makes leadership easier, even when you have to make the tough calls. Mary Poppins was right: a spoonful of sugar does help the medicine go down.

Kindness matters. In time, many people will forgive even the decisions that went against them if the leader demonstrates goodwill. Grouches, however, get little sympathy.

Kindness Comes from Confidence

I have found that in football officiating (and in many other circumstances) the less secure I am, the less kind I am. The more uncertain I am, the more defensive I am.

Early in my first season of officiating, on those occasions when I was a bit shaky about a call (rare occasions, of course), I would tense up and act extremely authoritative when a coach would question me. I noticed that, as the season progressed, I became more and more secure in my ability to listen calmly to coaches.

When I know the rule thoroughly, I can stand there like a gentleman even when the coach is displeased with my call. I'm learning that a level head and a prepared mind are a package deal.

So let's do our homework. Know who you are and what you are doing. Preparation breeds confidence. Confidence breeds serenity. And serenity breeds kindness.

Balancing Kindness

When I was a little boy, my mom told me the fable of a contest between the sun and the wind. They were arguing about who was the stronger, when along walked a man wearing a coat. The wind challenged the sun by saying, "I'll bet I can get his coat off him quicker than you can," and the sun accepted the challenge.

So, the wind blew and blew and blew until the man could hardly keep his feet. But the harder the wind blew, the more tightly the man pulled his coat around him. The wind finally gave up.

The sun then took his turn and began to shine gently on the man. The sun caressed the man with warmth until the man eventually removed his coat. The moral of the story is that warmth and gentleness are stronger than might and rage. It certainly is true of spiritual leadership.

Good leaders are not malicious. Ephesians 4:30–32 offers helpful words for the spiritual leader:

> *And do not grieve the Holy Spirit of God, with whom you were sealed for the day of redemption. Get rid of all bitterness, rage and anger, brawling and slander, along with every form of malice. Be kind and compassionate to one another, forgiving each other, just as in Christ God forgave you.*

The Bible also talks about "speaking the truth in love" (Ephesians 4:15). At times, leaders must correct and rebuke. So keep in mind that kindness is not the same as indulgence or lenience. There are two biblical values that must be kept in balance: compassion and accountability. John D. Beckett, a Christian and a business leader, writes in *Loving Monday*, "Compassion without accountability produces sentimentalism. Accountability without compassion is harsh and heartless."

In the story of the woman caught in adultery (John 8:1–11), Jesus had compassion on her and refused to take part in her stoning, yet he said to her, "Go and sin no more. (Don't do that again.)" The greatest leader in history balanced compassion with accountability.

Learning from the Master

Certainly, courageous and visionary decisions must be made, and inappropriate opposition has to be met head-on. But even when the Christian leader has legitimate grounds to confront, he or she should do so in love, with an attitude of humility and respect. Callousness is not an admirable trait for a spiritual leader.

"Jesus grew…in favor with God and men" (Luke 2:52). Of course not everyone embraced Him, but most who opposed Him opposed His teaching, His values, His convictions. As a person, He apparently gained widespread favor. People must have appreciated His tender heart when they heard Him say things like, "Don't keep those children from coming to me." Jesus must have been easy for the common person to love.

Unfortunately, too many Christians are failing in the gaining-people's-favor department. The reputation that Christians have as mean-spirited, unpleasant finger waggers is not completely undeserved. It is such a simple thing, but it would make a profound difference in our leadership if we would simply enjoy life and our neighbors a little more.

It is downright unchristian to be habitually disagreeable. It is downright unchristian to be sour, unpleasant, and vinegary.

It is downright unchristian to be a curmudgeon. If we Jesus-followers were a more positive, yes, even likable bunch, then our message might be better received.

And that kindness thing goes double for spiritual leaders. Sour dispositions are not very inspirational, and if you can't inspire people you are going to have a hard time leading them.

History has demonstrated no leadership quality more attractive than genuine, servant-like kindness. If you doubt that, ask the disciples who had their feet washed by the Master that Thursday night a couple of millennia ago.

Just for Vocational Ministers

Nastiness seems to be on the rise in some ministerial circles. I have heard pastors brag about the uproar they caused by making changes and then disparage those old spoilsports who opposed them. Some pastors have appeared proud of the number of people who have left the church. They have worn the number of defections like a badge of courage. They have collected those stories like the notches on a gunslinger's pearl-handled revolver.

That attitude disturbs me more than a little bit.

There seems to be a popular idea circulating in some circles—the idea that one cannot be compassionate and lead a church through necessary transitions. I fear such thinking is fostering a harshness among some ministers that is both unbecoming and unnecessary. I can't decide if this is a martyr complex, a messianic complex, or megalomania. One thing's for sure; it is over the top.

Ministerial authority does not mean that a pastor or other spiritual leader has the right to be an autocratic ruler. Nowhere does the Bible call us to be dictators. Nowhere does the Bible say that the leader is always right and the others are always wrong.

Could it be that some vocational ministers assume the domineering role out of fear or lack of confidence in their call or abilities? Church leadership expert Reggie McNeal thinks so. In *A Work of Heart* he writes, "Some leaders...claim to operate from 'spiritual authority' when in fact they are operating out of a deep sense of insecurity and lack of an overarching life mission." Insecure ministers are tempted to throw their weight around, even regarding small issues, thus alienating many people and making their own life unnecessarily difficult.

Good leaders aren't tyrants. And tyrants are not good leaders.

26

Moving On

When an official makes a mistake and knows it, he'd love to turn back the clock and try again—or he'd like to just disappear. He can't lose focus, though; he's got to immediately concentrate on the next play.

But it's not just officials who have to concentrate on the next play. If the quarterback throws three interceptions in the first half, he can't pack it up and go home. If the star forward misses a dunk or airballs a free throw, the game doesn't stop. Coaches too have to look ahead not backwards. They can't dwell on a loss or even a losing season.

Kodak formerly sponsored the annual college Coach of the Year award. At the awards banquet one year minister Sid Lovett prayed the "Loser's Prayer":

Thou art a God of mercy and so we lift before Thy care those coaches, who with endurance and honor but a losing record, are grateful for a new year. Deliver them from the nightmares of instant replay and sullen alumni. And if it

please Thee, bestow upon them surefingered ends, fleet
runners with secure cartilages, and linemen of granite.
—quoted in Calvin Miller's *The Empowered Leader*

There are a couple images from this prayer that catch my attention. The first is the image of a "new season." It's nice for someone who's had a tough go at it to end a rough season and begin anew with a clean slate. Maybe you have made some bad leadership choices and would like a "new season."

The second image is Lovett's reference to instant replay. "Deliver them from the nightmares of instant replay," he prayed. Now, instant replay is not all bad. It's good to look and learn from our bad choices. Reviewing the tape has its place. But there comes a time when the ref has to remove his head from under the drape and move on with the game.

Lessons from John Mark
Maybe you're having trouble moving away from the replay tape of some painful time in your life. In your mind you are replaying that mistake over and over and over. If you get one thing from this book let it be this: It's time to move on.

John Mark, my favorite New Testament character other than Jesus, took advantage of a "new season," and got on with life. He refused to let the instant replay of a youthful misstep prevent him from getting on with the game.

John Mark, most often just called "Mark," must have had a fascinating youth. Acts 12:12 says that Mark's mother, Mary, opened her home to the Jerusalem Christians. As a young man, Mark must have sat around soaking up the sagas recounted by Peter, James, and all those men and women who formed the

TOUGH CALLS

first core group of Christians. Then, when Paul and Barnabas prepared for their first missionary journey, John Mark signed on.

How it was that young Mark was invited to be a member of the team I don't know. Maybe it was because Barnabas and Mark were cousins (see Colossians 4:10). However it came to be, Mark kissed his mom goodbye and the illustrious missionary team embarked on their adventures.

At first it must have been exciting for Mark. Seeing new places. Learning from Paul and Barnabas. Knowing that people at home were praying for him and missing him. Maybe feeling a little bit like a hero.

But something happened along the way. We don't know the whole story—there are numerous possibilities—but we do know that in a place called Pamphylia, John Mark went AWOL. Left and went home. Paul and Barnabas completed their journey Mark-less.

If this were a movie, the following words would now flash across the bottom of the screen: "Several years later." Several years have passed since the day John Mark abandoned Paul and Barnabas. Several years have passed since Paul was so put out with Mark that he wouldn't give him another chance.

The camera escorts us into a cold, dark, musty prison cell and there sits an aged and worn Apostle Paul in the corner. A candle illumines the parchment on which he writes. He has come down to the last mile, and he obviously is contemplating his impending martyrdom. Paul writes, in the letter we call Second Timothy, "I have fought a good fight, I have finished the race, I have kept the faith."

A couple of sentences later he tells Timothy, "Bring Mark to me, for he is a big help to me."

Wait. Did he say *Mark*? "Bring *Mark* to me?"

We would not have been surprised if Paul had written, "When you come bring anybody you want except that quitter, John Mark." But something had happened. Maybe John Mark went to Paul one day, apologized, and asked for Paul's forgiveness. Or maybe Paul watched carefully as John Mark served, first under Barnabas, and then in other capacities, even alongside Paul himself. Maybe years after their big split, Paul went to John Mark one day and said, "I have watched you grow and mature. I've watched you become a Christian leader. And you have made me very proud."

We all have things in our pasts of which we are ashamed. But we don't have to let a burden of shame keep us from moving on to better things.

Young Mark picked himself up, dusted himself off, and proved his mettle on that second missionary journey with Barnabas. He later served alongside other church leaders, wrote a Gospel, and ministered to Paul while Paul was imprisoned in Rome. Paul came to consider him a useful and encouraging colaborer. In short, Mark moved on.

Try, Try Again

Countless are the stories of executive decision-makers who once failed miserably but then turned out to be stellar leaders. In many cases, the leaders were terminated by one organization and then excelled in another. Numerous times discredited leaders have prevailed despite the protests of colleagues who said they didn't deserve another chance. Those who overcome serious setbacks have been courageous enough to learn from their errors and bold enough to get back on the horse that threw them.

- Steve Jobs was one of Apple's two cofounders, but some of the employees complained about his leadership style, and Jobs clashed with the CEO he himself had recruited—John Scully. Eventually Jobs was relieved of his duties as the head of the Macintosh division—his pride and joy—and found himself outside the inner circle of the company he had founded. That was too much, and he left the company he'd gotten off the ground. After founding NeXT Computer, however, Jobs made a comeback. Twelve years after his unceremonious departure from Apple, he returned to lead the company, which now enjoys enormous success.

- Kurt Warner tried out for the Green Bay Packers in 1994, but was told thanks, but no thanks. A year later he was stocking supermarket shelves in Cedar Rapids, Iowa, when he got a second chance at football, in the Arena Football League (AFL). He then went from the AFL's Iowa Barnstormers to NFL Europe to backup quarterback for the St. Louis Rams. Warner became the Rams' starter early in the 1999 season after an injury to Trent Green. He led the Rams to a Super Bowl victory that year and earned the NFL's MVP award. In 2001 Warner again was named MVP of the league, and the Rams went back to the Super Bowl, losing a close one to the New England Patriots.

- In April 1978 the board of directors of Handy Dan, a small chain of home improvement stores, fired their CEO, Bernie Marcus. On that same day they fired another Handy Dan employee named Arthur Blank. Rather than lament their misfortune in an unemployment line, Marcus and Blank decided to start their own hardware store. They've been fairly successful, I'd say. The hardware giant, Home Depot, is the result of their visionary collaboration.

- Mike Flynt blew it. He got in trouble for fighting one too many times, and administrators at Sul Ross State grew tired of messing with this talented but out-of-control jock. Mike, a member of the football team, was sent packing just before his senior year.

  With maturity came regret, and one day when he was reminiscing with his old football buddies, they suggested that if he really did want another shot at it, he ought to go back to school. Mike found out he had a year of eligibility left, and asked for the opportunity to try out for the team back at Sul Ross State, a Division-III school in Alpine, Texas.

  Sure enough, that year of eligibility was waiting for him. Of course the fact that he was eligible didn't mean he would make the team; he'd been out of football for a while. Out of football long enough, in fact, to have children . . . and grandchildren. Flynt was 59 years old (no, that is not a typo) when he made the team the second time *and* played in 2007.

I love Isaiah 54:4–5, where we read, "You will forget the shame of your youth . . . for . . . the Holy One of Israel is your Redeemer." Remember that a "redeemer" is one who takes something useless and turns it into something valuable. I love that verse, for God has redeemed some of those things I'm not so proud of from my youth. I might just look up Mark one day and ask him if maybe that was his favorite verse, as well.

Perhaps one day you, too, will tell the story of how you decided not to be shackled to your mistakes and allowed God to redeem your past. In the meantime, let's move on and, in the words of Jesus, be about "our Father's business."

Just for Vocational Ministers

Certain sinful choices disqualify us for vocational ministry, at least for a season. The health, integrity, and reputation of the church sometimes require a fallen pastor to resign.

However, if (and only if) that person has owned his or her sin, has made necessary restitution, and has sought both forgiveness and healing, then it might be appropriate (depending on the situation, the nature of the transgression, and the mental/spiritual health of the fallen minister) for that person to step back into a formal position of church leadership.

Most of our mistakes, thankfully, are not so severe that they require our resignation. Most of our mistakes require only an honest acknowledgement of the blunder and a deep determination to move on.

27

Make the Call—
It's Your Job

We're back to where we started. Leadership is about tough calls, and you've gotta make 'em. It's your job.

In my previous book, *Directionally Challenged*, I told this story about a tough call I had to make one evening when I was officiating a football game between two local high schools.

The ball carrier came my way, and I followed him down the sideline, glancing from side to side looking for holds or clips or other potential fouls. My primary responsibility, however, was to keep my eye on the runner and the ball.

When the runner was tackled, several yards downfield, I saw right where he fell. There was only one problem; he had fallen with his back toward me, and when he rolled over he didn't have the ball! He had been running with it, but he no longer possessed it. I looked back about five yards, and there was a player from the other team with the ball in his hand. It was obvious the runner didn't have it when he hit the ground, but I had no idea how the other player had gotten it.

A second official arrived on the scene and I asked him, "Did you see what happened?" He hadn't. But we reasoned that the only thing that could have happened was that the runner was stripped of the ball before he fell, back around the spot where the player from the other team stood holding the ball. It was the only thing that made sense.

So I made a call. I gave the ball to the defensive team, first down, at the spot where the player was holding it. (The young man who'd been carrying the ball didn't complain, so I figured we probably had gotten it right.) Well, the fans went berserk. The coach went berserker! I looked a bit like I didn't know what I was doing, I'll admit. And I had to make a decision based on insufficient information. But I had to make a decision.

One of the primary responsibilities of an official is to make a decision and live with it. And yes, there are times when blowing the whistle and throwing the flag are tough. Judgment calls can be stressful. Throwing a penalty flag when I'm standing right in front of the offending team's coach, for example, isn't easy. But if there ever comes a night when I can't bring myself to make those calls, I will resign the following morning.

Decision making is how we earn our stripes as leaders. The one thing that sets the leader apart is decision making; decision making is the point at which one's leadership is usually made or broken.

Leadership, therefore, boils down not only to the ability, but also the willingness, to make difficult decisions.

Don't Be a Mugwump

In the NFL, the officials are evaluated weekly and meticulously. In days gone by, the officials were graded on a seven-point scale, with seven being the best. According to that grading system, an official could receive the highest grade—seven— if he made an accurate call in a tough situation. If the official made a good call that was obvious to even the casual fan, then he might have gotten a five. But a *tough* call was worth *more*, recalls former official Jim Tunney in his book *Impartial Judgment*.

When you make a tough-but-accurate call, people will grade you highly, too. Oh, they might not say anything about it, but they will notice. At least some of them will. People know it when the leader is making a difficult decision, and many will appreciate your willingness to make the call whether they agree with it or not. And when you make a tough call that proves to be a correct call, you will earn a lot of leadership capital in the organization.

Respect is earned by making the tough calls. It is when people in the organization say, "I wouldn't want to be in your shoes," that you truly become the leader. When everyone knows the decision is not clear-cut, and that no matter what you do someone is going to be unhappy, your value to the organization becomes obvious. People are glad to follow a leader they can trust to make courageous, principled decisions.

Whether you are a sports official or a spiritual leader, you can't be, in a word, a "mugwump." I'll never forget this imagined letter from Calvin Miller's *The Empowered Leader*:

Dear Leader:

It was Miss Smith, my third grade teacher that first taught me about mugwumps. They're real hard to describe, so I won't try. It's just enough that you know that they spend all of their lives straddling fences. I can't imagine a more neurotic way to live, can you? . . .

I know why mugwumps avoid decision making. Deciding is risky. Every single time you do it, you run the risk of being wrong. Of course, you also have a wonderful opportunity of being right. Either way, however, deciding seems to me less frustrating than having to live in that self-imposed state of paralysis known as decidophobia . . .

[M]ake a decision and take off. I'll follow you even if your decision is wrong. I'd just as soon go the wrong direction now and then, as never go anywhere.
—Your Follower

I have loved Miller's letter since I first read it. Yet I really didn't understand what a mugwump was until a couple of years later when, out of the blue, a lady in our church told me that her daddy used to say, "Don't be like a mugwump, 'cause a mugwump always has his mug on one side of the fence and his wump on the other!"

Mugwumps make poor sports officials and poor Christian leaders. People will not respect someone who is unable to make the tough calls necessary for success. If you avoid the tough calls, people will notice. Influence is lost when decisions are evaded.

Of course capricious decisions don't serve anyone well. Tough calls are to be made courageously, but not haphazardly. There are right and wrong ways to make tough calls. Options and risks must be weighed. Timing, long-term consequences, and systemic issues must be considered. The leader's own motives must be evaluated. Then, in the end, the hard decisions must be made.

Not everyone is cut out to be a sports official, and not everyone is cut out to be a leader. The ability to make tough decisions without developing instant ulcers is one of the distinguishing marks of the ability to serve in a leadership role.

You've got to make the call...even the tough one. It's your job.

Listen for His Voice

Easier said than done, you say?

Well, I hope that the stories and principles in this book will be of some use to you as you wrestle with difficult decisions in the future. And I want to make two final points.

First, as a leader, trust your instincts. Your instincts are the accumulation of experiences you've had. And you must have picked up some wisdom and knowledge over the years, or else you wouldn't be in leadership at all. You might not be able to articulate *why* you think something should or should not be done, but chances are there are some subconscious calculations going on that give you the sense about what should happen in a situation. Your instincts will not always be right, but you're going to have to trust them and then live with your decisions when there is no clear-cut right or wrong.

Second, as a spiritual leader you have a resource far more powerful than your instincts. God's Spirit has called you and is more concerned about your effectiveness than you are. Thus it is possible to stand at those many crossroads of leadership and know which way to turn. God promised us, "Whether you turn to the right or the left, your ears will hear a voice behind you saying, 'This is the way; walk in it" (Isaiah 30:21).

I was driving in New York City a few years ago with two church staff members, Valerie Carter and Julia Wilmouth, in the backseat. They knew where we were going; I didn't. They didn't tell me the entire route at the beginning; I couldn't have understood that. They would, however, tell me where to go just in time for me to get into the correct lane and make the appropriate turns. I kept in contact with them. They were close by. And they pointed the way.

At the beginning of our journey God doesn't usually reveal all the twists and turns we will encounter. But I do believe that when it comes time to make a decision, He will whisper, "This is the way; walk in it." I am mystical enough to believe that the Spirit of God will say to those called as spiritual leaders, "This is the right direction for the organization you lead."

Just for Vocational Ministers

Not many of us in vocational ministry have the sole responsibility for making the big decisions. Most of us lead by leading the decision-makers, whether elders, a bishop, or the congregation itself. Nevertheless, it is your behind-the-scenes decisions that set the stage for the calls your church makes.

Authori*tarian* leadership (the minister is boss) should be rejected. Authori*tative* leadership (the minister speaks and lives with contagious conviction and vision), however, is the kind of leadership that results in strong churches. Even those with authority to make the final decisions are going to look to you for direction. When they do, you're going to have to make the call. It's your job.

CONCLUSION

The Closing Minutes

There is a growing shortage of sports officials, and the increasingly intense harassment we receive is undoubtedly part of the problem. In a survey by the National Association of Sports Officials, state high school sports administrators cited poor sportsmanship by spectators as the number one reason officials quit. The next most frequently mentioned reason was poor sportsmanship by coaches and players.

I'm certain that countless leaders also quit because of their disappointment with the behavior of those they lead. Most leaders with whom I speak find personnel issues to be the primary source of their headaches and heartaches. And those in customer service or retail often find people to be unreasonable and caustic. Budgets, growth strategies, and endless meetings don't cause nearly as much frustration as people do.

Our son, Landon, studied leadership in college, so I asked him to read the first draft of this book. In one of the margins toward the end of the manuscript he wrote, "Is there any hope for Christian leaders?" I certainly didn't intend to paint a bleak picture of spiritual leadership in this book. I did, however, intend to be realistic, at least as I see it. The naked truth is that leadership is no easy task, even when we are doing our best to lead as Jesus led. Leadership is hard because leadership is "people business," and disappointment in people makes throwing in the towel seem awfully tempting.

Monkeys Everywhere

Do you ever daydream about leaving your job? Just walking away? Finding greener grass? Going to where the people are easier to work with?

Sound attractive right now?

Well, leaving is not often the best choice.

Recently CareerBuilder.com has produced several funny television commercials. The commercials show a guy in an office full of monkeys. In one of the commercials, the monkeys are toying with the copier, playing computer games, and monkeying around at the water cooler. While apologizing to a client on the phone for the ineptitude of his company, the one human employee in the office says, "I'm sorry, but...I work with a bunch of monkeys." Then the question pops up: "Want a better job?" The implied message is, "Let us help you find that place to work where there are no monkeys."

But here's the truth: there are monkeys everywhere.

There is no perfect workplace. There is no perfect school. There is no perfect community. There is no perfect church. There is no perfect team. There are no perfect relationships.

Maybe you are tempted to leave your place of leadership—tempted to circulate your resume among other companies. That might be the right thing; sometimes our personal values so conflict with the values of our present place of service that we cannot remain there. But leaving is usually not the answer, and it never should be the default plan. Don't let disappointment with people become something that drives you away, for you are likely to face that same disappointment in your next place of leadership as well. Leaving often is a shortsighted, short-lived solution. After all, there are monkeys everywhere.

Don't Throw in the Towel Just Yet

Paul, the missionary, began his letter to Timothy, his protégé, with an interesting mandate: "As I urged you when I went into Macedonia, stay there in Ephesus" (1 Timothy 1:3). Timothy was young at the time and perhaps easily discouraged. There certainly were plenty of things to be discouraged about in Ephesus, and the people Timothy was leading were his biggest problem.

The Ephesian church was a somewhat troublesome group of relatively new and spiritually immature Christians. Many had wild and heretical beliefs; indeed the influence of idol worship was strong in the city and made its way into the church. Many were skeptical of Timothy's leadership abilities. Because of his youth and inexperience, and because he had the difficult task of following that superb leader named Paul, the folks at Ephesus apparently were looking down their noses at Timothy (see 1 Timothy 4:12; 2 Timothy 2:6–8).

Perhaps Timothy had expressed openly to Paul his desire to leave those recalcitrant malcontents—to move to greener pastures—to go to an easier assignment where the people were better humored. But Paul said, "Timothy, stay in Ephesus."

Some of you are tempted to leave your present positions, and others of you are tempted to leave leadership altogether. How many of us have longed for a 9-to-5 job in which we can leave the work at the office? How many of us have secretly desired, at least fleetingly, to trade the business suit for the greeter's vest at Wal-Mart? How many of us have longed for any way of making a decent living in which we'll never have to make another decision and never have to supervise another soul? I know a man who used to be high in the personnel department of a large company. He retired early and now works in the produce department at a grocery store. "I love the vegetables," he says. "They are so much easier to work with than people."

Many of you could have written this book better than I, for you have survived and thrived in more difficult situations than those I have known. I have been blessed, and with few exceptions, those I have led and served alongside have been people of stellar character with a passion for God's mission.

I know that many of you have suffered painful attacks, and that some of you are living through assaults right now. Despite the circumstances, my closing desire for you is that you will not quit. The world needs your gifts of leadership.

Obviously there are situations in which one's health, the well-being of one's family, and even the good of the organization, make resignation appropriate. Yet the need for leaders of deep spirituality and unshakable integrity is so great that none of us should step away hastily. And if you have to step away from your present position of leadership, we need you to find another place of leadership soon. Our world needs leaders of faith and character.

Worth It

Spiritual leadership is a privileged calling. Despite the rigors of our callings—whatever and wherever they may be—this really is a blessed life. The opportunity for positive influence in people's lives is a gift. Despite our sins and limitations, God in His mercy has allowed us to be spiritual leaders. We know a sense of purpose that some people never find.

If you will take the time to look back on your life of leadership, I'm guessing that you, too, will see the blessings in your service. If you dig beneath the anguish of your tough calls, you will find a satisfaction that comes only with the opportunity of leadership.

In chapter six, "Battle Scars," I quoted Max De Pree, who compared the wounds and scars of a leader to the skinned knees, elbows, and shins of a boy at the end of an adventuresome summer. Ann Perkins, professor of leadership studies at Christopher Newport University, read the first draft of this book and wrote in the margins next to De Pree's comments:

> *The six-year-old boy at the end of August has had a great time getting those bruises and scars, and he is proud of every one of them. So too a leader. Leadership is hard and it may leave you punch-drunk, but the true leader can look back on the experience and say it was worth it.*

Spiritual leaders, you are investing in priceless human lives and in great causes, the return from which you might not see this side of Heaven. So keep on investing yourself and maybe, somehow, at the end of the journey God will let you witness the difference you have made and cannot yet see. Maybe, just before He ushers you into Heaven, God will give you a glimpse of the people whose lives were transformed for good and forever on account of you and your willingness to make the tough calls. And then, best of all, He will be there to greet you, His faithful—though perhaps weary—servant.

> *"So we fix our eyes not on what is seen, but on what is unseen. For what is seen is temporary, but what is unseen is eternal."*
> —2 Corinthians 4:1

Tough Calls
Discussion Questions

One day my friend, Glenn Akins, saw me working on the manuscript for *Tough Calls* and asked what I was doing. After I explained the book he suggested, "Why don't you provide some materials for people to discuss at lunch, before work, or in some kind of small-group setting?" Glenn believed this might help Christ-followers integrate their faith with their daily work. Below is my answer to Glenn's suggestion—group discussion questions for each section. It is my prayerful hope that this book and these questions will be helpful to you as you seek to be salt and light in the world. Working through these questions in a group setting and discussing appropriate applications can only broaden each participant's perspective and stimulate further thought.

Vocational ministers should also find these questions helpful. I can imagine a group of my colleagues reading the book and discussing it in weekly church staff meetings, at a staff retreat, or among ministry friends who gather for support and personal development. The sections in the book specifically targeted to minister-types should especially provide fertile ground for lively discussion.

In each case, participants should read the section beforehand and come prepared to dialogue about the questions. A spirit of openness and honesty will benefit everyone. I believe you can cover these questions thoroughly in less than an hour.

Thank you for reading this book as part of your spiritual development. I hope it has strengthened your desire and ability to emulate Jesus, even in making tough calls.

—Travis Collins

Section One

1. How do you define *leadership*, and how can you exercise leadership in your present role(s)?
2. Review the leadership qualities of Jesus highlighted in the introduction. Can you think of other characteristics of Jesus's leadership?
3. Discuss a recent tough call that you had to make. Did your faith shape the way you made that call?
4. Tell about a time when you really blew it as a leader. Have you been able to move on from that, or are you still dragging that memory around?

Section Two

1. I write in chapter 6 that war stories come with the leadership territory. This would be a good time to share your best war stories with your fellow leaders.
2. Leaders prove their mettle in crisis. Tell of a time when you had to lead your organization through difficult times.
3. Go back and read the story of the goldfish in chapter 8. How do you find the balance to ensure your organization is neither stifled by traditionalism nor traumatized by reckless change?
4. Review the questions suggested in chapter 8 for those who are initiating change. Could you add your own helpful questions?

Section Three

1. Describe a time when you saw a leader exhibit the kind of poise you read about in this section.
2. Discuss "emotional intelligence" (see chapter 9). Did you learn something from these chapters that will help keep you from saying or doing something you might later regret?
3. Discuss "self-differentiation" (see chapter 11). You might have to do a bit of research online. How can this concept help you maintain poise?

4. If poise really is rooted in spiritual disciplines, how are you doing in this area? Are you taking the time to refresh your soul and connect with your Creator?

Section Four

1. Is it really possible to avoid taking criticism personally (see chapter 13)? How will this section help you to view criticism a bit more objectively?
2. Can you remember a time when you listened to criticism and you shouldn't have? What about a time when you should have listened to criticism and didn't?
3. I write, "Peace at any cost is not worth the cost." Do you think Jesus taught that? Can you think of a time when the mission of an organization was compromised because of an inordinate desire that people get along?
4. Does your desire to have people like you ever hamper your leadership? How can you overcome that without becoming calloused?

Section Five

1. In chapter 17 I write about the difference between "malice" and "appropriate debate and disagreement." How would you distinguish between the two?
2. Discuss a time when you avoided a confrontation and now regret it. What about a time when you feel you confronted in a timely and appropriate way? What were the results?
3. Some people say, "If you just give them time, most problems work themselves out." Is there wisdom in waiting? When does patience become avoidance? Does every problem "work itself out"?
4. Is there someone under your leadership who should be terminated? Is there a legitimate reason for your hesitancy? What steps must precede termination? How can you make this somehow redemptive for both the organization and the individual?

Section Six

1. What obligation do you think team members have to leave their disagreements in the conference room? Are people in your organization free to disagree with team decisions? Should they be?
2. In chapter 21 Peter Drucker is quoted: "One hears a great deal today about 'the end of hierarchy.' This is blatant nonsense." Do you agree with Drucker? Aren't we supposed to be moving toward flat organizations? Is a chain of command necessary?
3. Are you a "second-chair leader" (see chapter 22)? Have you found anything in this chapter that will help you better exercise leadership from your position in the organization?
4. How has your position of leadership been hard on your family? Are there things you can do to lessen the negative impact on them? You may want to take the time to pray for each other's families.

Section Seven

1. Do you tend first to assume that the responsibility for conflict rests with the other party? What are some characteristics of your personality that might heighten interpersonal tension if you aren't careful?
2. In chapter 25 John Beckett is quoted: "Compassion without accountability produces sentimentalism. Accountability without compassion is harsh and heartless." How are you able to strike that balance?
3. Are you willing to talk openly about a failure and the lessons you have learned from it?
4. Talk about the danger of being a "mugwump" (see chapter 27).
5. In the conclusion there is a quotation from Ann Perkins: "Leadership is hard and it may leave you punch-drunk, but the true leader can look back on the experience and say it was worth it." Wrap up your group discussion by sharing your joys and rewards from spiritual leadership.

Make the Right Call
with These Books on Leadership